P9-BIH-980

Palm Springs Modern

BY ADÈLE CYGELMAN · FOREWORD BY JOSEPH ROSA · PHOTOGRAPHS BY DAVID GLOMB

PALM SPRINGS MODERN

Houses in the California Desert

RIZZOLI
NEW YORK

First published in the United States of America in 1999 by

Rizzoli International Publications, Inc.

300 Park Avenue South, New York, NY 10010

Copyright ©1999 Rizzoli International Publications, Inc.

All rights reserved. No part of this publication may be reproduced in any manner

whatsoever without permission in writing from Rizzoli International Publications, Inc.

ISBN 0-8478-2091-2

LC 98-48811

Design by Alison Hahn and Nigel Smith at Hahn Smith Design, Toronto. Design Associate: Sara Soskolne

Printed and bound in Singapore

Jacket front: The pool of the Raymond Loewy House, viewed from the living room. (see page 38)

Jacket back: The Kaufmann House, 1947. (photograph by Julius Shulman, see page 63)

Inside flap: The Loewy House, 1957. (photograph by Charles Herbert, see page 16)

Title page: Early morning in the hills of Little Tuscany, looking down at the city of Palm Springs and toward the Santa Rosa Mountains.

Preceding pages: Twilight poolside at Frank Sinatra's first desert home in the north end of Palm Springs. (see page 72)

Note: We used "Palm Springs" as shorthand for an area that also embraces Cathedral City, Rancho Mirage, Palm Desert, Indian Wells, La Quinta, Indio, and Desert Hot Springs. To the residents of those cities, we intended no slight, just a desire to keep the title short.

Contents

Acknowledgments

David and I thank the following people for making this project possible at every stage of its development:

Julius Shulman; Doug Smith and the pool at Korakia Pensione; Elizabeth McMillian; David Morton and Rizzoli International Publications; Stewart Weiner of *Palm Springs Life*; and Tony Merchell, without whom none of this would have been imagined.

We have barged (sometimes unannounced) into people's lives and tramped through a multitude of rooms on our journey. I hope this book conveys our gratitude to an extraordinary group of individuals who shared their houses with gracious hospitality and patience: Ambassador and Mrs. Walter H. Annenberg, Hal Broderick, William and Clara Burgess, Stanley and Deburha Clark, Marjorie Edris, Albert Frey, Jim Gaudineer and Tony Padilla, Brent and Beth Harris, Gordon Locksley and Dr. George Shea, Luella Maslon, Katharine O. Mavis, Jim Moore, Max Palevsky, Marc Sanders, E. Stewart and the late Mari Williams.

For their invaluable input: Donald Wexler, Margaret Roades, and the librarians at the Palm Springs Public Library, Sally McManus of the Palm Springs Historical Society, Carl Prout of the Palm Springs Historic Site Preservation Foundation, the Palm Springs Desert Museum, Nan Tynberg, John J. Cody, Lynne Cody, Catherine Cody, George Hasslein, Russell Wade, Marvin Roos, Lorraine and Robert Moore, the Modern Committee of the Los Angeles Conservancy, Elaine K. S. Jones, William Ezelle Jones, Laurel Mugling, Piper Mavis, Marion Jorgensen, Thomas Riedel.

And to our partners in crime: Bob Moore and Marcello Villano.

Adèle Cygelman

Concentric stone circles balance the angularity of the low-lying house A. Quincy Jones designed for the Chicago-based Robinson family. (see page 124)

9

Foreword

It was good to be in California.... You couldn't feel safe anywhere, except in the desert....
— Henry Miller, *The Air-Conditioned Nightmare*

The notion of the desert as a secure haven from the realities of everyday life is best typified in Henry Miller's *The Air-Conditioned Nightmare*, published in 1945. Moreover, as the title suggests, with the advent of air-conditioning the cultural landscape of the desert changed from an arid, sparsely populated terrain to a viable destination spot for the second homes of the post–World War II leisure class. To understand the evolution of postwar modern domestic architecture in Palm Springs, however, one must look at what preceded it.

The modern idiom was, in fact, prevalent in the desert prior to 1940. There were designs by noted architects from Los Angeles and the East Coast — mostly immigrants — who were disciples of world-renowned architects such as Louis Sullivan, Frank Lloyd Wright, and Le Corbusier. The first house to be built in the modern idiom in the desert region of California was by a Los Angeles–based Frank Lloyd Wright disciple, Rudolph M. Schindler. His 1922 Popenoe Cabin, built in the Coachella region of the desert, was constructed of materials such as concrete, wood, and canvas, and was reminiscent of Schindler's own house built in Los Angeles in the same year.[1] His only other built design for the desert was the 1946 Toole House in Palm Village, which was designed in a more organic idiom of wood and stone that gave it a rather heavy appearance. William Gray Purcell, a disciple of Louis Sullivan, designed a weekend retreat for himself in Palm Springs in 1933 with Evera Van Bailey

At the Edgar J. Kaufmann House an ocotillo cactus stands in front of the "gloriette," Richard Neutra's term for the open second-story living area. (see page 50)

(fig. 1). The house is designed in the Prairie School idiom with modifications to make it fit in to the desert region.[2] Richard J. Neutra's first residential commission for the desert was his 1937 Miller House in Palm Springs (fig. 2). The Miller House, also known as the "Mensendieck" House, was designed for Grace Lewis Miller, a recent widow and teacher of the Mensendieck System of Functional Exercise in St. Louis. In 1936, shortly after the death of her husband, Mrs. Miller decided to open a Mensendieck studio in the health-conscious environment of California and settled on a site in Palm Springs—near the affluent Racquet Club—where she lived, seasonally, and taught.[3] The Miller House was Neutra's best small house of the 1930s and it was included in the 1938 Museum of Modern Art traveling exhibition on modern domestic architecture.[4] In the early 1930s there were a few Art Deco–style homes in Palm Springs, but nothing as grand as the 1936 Davidson House designed by Los Angeles architects Eric Webster and Adrian Wilson (fig. 3). This seasonal 4,000-square-foot house was built for the prominent Davidson family of Washington, D.C. However, shortly after the completion of the house, Mrs. Davidson learned of her husband's infidelity and took her own life.[5] This extensive hillside house, designed in the idiom of streamline modern, featured some of the most progressive window detailing in America at the time. The most innovative detail was the living-room windows. The curved edge of the living room had sweeping views of the desert beyond; with windows set in metal frames that were counter-weighted and pocketed down into the window sill to completely disappear from view. The window detailing in the Davidson House was very similar to that of Ludwig Mies van der Rohe's 1930 Tugendhat House in Brno, Czechoslovakia, where a complete wall of glass disappears into the floor.

Concurrently, East Coast firms were also designing modern homes for the desert region. The New York–based firm of A. Lawrence Kocher, then managing editor of *Architectural Record*, and Albert Frey, the first disciple of Le Corbusier to build in America, designed the Kocher-Samson Building in 1934 (fig. 4). The building was designed for Kocher's brother Dr. J. J. Kocher, the first doctor to live and practice in the desert. It was one of the few modern buildings located on Palm Springs's main thoroughfare, North Palm Canyon Drive. Photographs of this modern office with an apartment above were shown at the Museum of Modern Art exhibition "Modern Architecture in California" in October 1935, which also featured the works of Richard J. Neutra, R. M. Schindler, William Wurster, and A. C. Zimmerman. The exhibition catalogue cited the Kocher-Samson building as being "typical of the restrained ingenuity of the eastern experimentalism which in contrast with that of California seems economical and chaste." Kocher and Frey were the only architects in the exhibition not based in California, although they were among the first architects to build on both coasts in the modern idiom, and theirs was the only contribution to the exhibition that was built in Palm Springs.[6] Furthermore, the architectural historian David Gebhard has called the Kocher-Samson Building "the most pure example of the international style [building] in Southern California."[7]

Although the collaboration between Walter Gropius and Marcel Breuer only lasted a few years, from 1937 to 1941, they produced some of the best early examples of modern domestic architecture in America. During this period Gropius was chair of the school of architecture at Harvard University, and Breuer was a professor at the school. The houses they

Fig 1. Purcell House, Palm Springs, 1933, William Gray Purcell and Evera Van Bailey

Fig 3. Davidson House, Palm Springs, 1936, Eric Webster and Adrian Wilson

Fig 2. Grace Lewis Miller House, Palm Springs, 1938, Richard Neutra

Fig 4. Kocher-Samson Building, Palm Springs, 1934, A. Lawrence Kocher and Albert Frey

Fig 5. Frey House 1, Palm Springs, 1940, Albert Frey

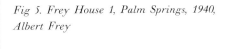

13

designed became the models from which later modern residential designs were measured. Most of these houses were designed for the East Coast. However, the architects also designed the Margoulis House in 1938–39 for the desert terrain of Palm Springs, but it was never built due to the clients' divorce.[8] Because the architects' houses had become so influential in the East, one can only wonder how this one might have influenced the course of modern architecture in Palm Springs had it been built.

The most significant partnership in the desert, however, was the collaboration between John Porter Clark and Albert Frey—the first modern architects to live and practice in Palm Springs. Clark, known as the first architect of the desert, was born in Iowa, raised in California, and educated at Cornell University in upstate New York. Frey was born in Zurich, Switzerland, educated at the Institute of Technology in Winterthur, and moved from New York City to Palm Springs in 1934 to supervise the construction of the Kocher-Samson Building. Attracted to the landscape, Frey decided to stay and ended his partnership with A. Lawrence Kocher in New York, met Clark, and started a partnership that lasted for almost twenty years. The collaboration lasted from 1935 to 1937 and again in 1939 through 1956. However, their official arrival in the desert was marked by the design and construction of their own homes—Clark's in 1939 (see page 28) and Frey's in 1940 (fig. 5)—which were both wood-framed, flat-roofed, and sheathed in corrugated metal.[9] Prior to this, most of the modern houses in the desert, with the exception of Schindler's 1922 Popenoe Cabin, while also wood-framed, were sheathed in the more standard wire lath and stucco, the same material used on the more traditionally styled houses in the desert. The actual sheathing of a wood-framed structure with corrugated metal challenged the normative building vocabulary while furthering the notion of the house, as Le Corbusier would say, as a "Machine for Living" in rugged terrain. Clark and Frey's homes were important contributions toward placing Palm Springs's domestic architecture on the map as a new frontier for the modern idiom, appearing in magazines such as *Architectural Forum*, *Architectural Record*, *Domus*, *House and Garden*, *Werk*, and in books such as *The Modern House in America* by Katherine and James Ford, and *A Decade of New Architecture*, edited by Sigfried Giedion.

E. Stewart Williams arrived in Palm Springs in 1946 and William E. Cody in 1945. Together Clark, Frey, Williams, and Cody set the tone for the practice of mid-century modern architecture in Palm Springs. The development of air-conditioning in the postwar years made Palm Springs a viable leisure resort town for the affluent. Over the next three decades, building in Palm Springs flourished from domestic to civic scale, and modern architecture was prevalent. But despite the fact that it took the desert years to become a mecca for modern design, in the late 1970s tastes changed and the modern aesthetic was no longer in favor.

Since the 1990s, however, Palm Springs has been rediscovered by a culturally ambitious younger set. The homes have become—once again—desirable. Thanks to people in the film, design, and fashion industries, many houses have been purchased in the past few years and are now restored or being restored. The same is also true for modern houses of the 1930s that predate the later ones, such as the Miller and Davidson houses. Historically, Palm Springs has finally come into its own. Today mid-century modern architecture in the desert is equated with the late-1970s discovery and preservation of Art Deco architecture in

Miami Beach. It is only a matter of time before the Palm Springs Historical Society fully acknowledges these buildings as significant contributions to the history of the desert, and to American architecture. Although a few buildings have been landmarked, none is listed in the official *Palm Springs Historic Architectural Highlights* guidebook. More importantly, one cannot forget the role the modern idiom has played in establishing the mid-century notion of Palm Springs as the arid, surreal terrain for leisure and escape from the realities of everyday modern life.

Joseph Rosa

Endnotes

1. David Gebhard. *Schindler* (Salt Lake City: Peregrine Smith, Inc., 1980) 51–2.

2. David Gebhard and Robert Winter. *A Guide to Architecture in Southern California* (Los Angeles: Los Angeles County Museum of Art, 1965) 140.

3. See Stephen Leet's forthcoming book on the Neutra's Miller House, *Richard Neutra, The Miller [Mensendieck] House*, to be published by Princeton Architectural Press in 1999.

4. Thomas S. Hines. *Richard Neutra and the Search for Modern Architecture.* (New York: Oxford University Press, 1982) 120.

5. "A Home Plan that Includes the Furniture," *Sunset* (October 1937) 31–2; Marian Montgomery and Yvonne Johnson. "Grand Estates," *Palm Springs Life* (May 1983) 26–7.

6. Joseph Rosa. *Albert Frey, Architect* (New York: Rizzoli International Publications, 1990) 35–6.

7. David Gebhard and Robert Winter. 140.

8. Winfried Nerdinger. *Walter Gropius* (Berlin: Gebr. Mann Verlag, 1985) 271.

9. Joseph Rosa. 36–7, 70–1.

Illustrations

1. Courtesy: UCSB Art Museum, The University of California at Santa Barbara

2. Julius Shulman

3. *Sunset* Magazine

4. Stephen Willard

5. Julius Shulman

CHARLES HERBERT

*Industrial designer Raymond Loewy, his wife, Viola, and
their daughter, Laurence, in the free-form pool of their Albert
Frey–designed home, 1957. (see page 38)*

Forget Las Vegas

Forget Las Vegas.

Palm Springs in the 1940s and 1950s was where Hollywood really came to play. And they rarely played in public. They didn't need to. They had the privacy of their own walled estates or gated country clubs.

The stars came to get a tan poolside at the Desert Inn, play tennis at the Racquet Club, go horseback riding into Tahquitz Canyon, shop at I. Magnin, drink martinis at the Bamboo Bar or the Doll House and dance to Louis Armstrong's orchestra at the Chi Chi. Palm Springs became synonymous with Bob Hope, Frank Sinatra, and Dinah Shore. Palm Springs meant fun in the sun, golf, and *Palm Springs Weekend*. It has always seemed an idyllic if superficial playground for Hollywood and the social set. And yet under that hedonistic haze lies a city with very sophisticated architectural roots.

From the 1930s to the 1960s, Palm Springs prospered. Movie stars, presidents, business tycoons, and artists descended from November to April on the new winter resort of choice. Reservations at El Mirador, the Desert Inn, or Oasis hotels were a must. Many frustrated visitors who couldn't get a hotel room would return, buy land, and build their own vacation house.

The first grand estates built in the 1920s and 1930s in the Las Palmas and Movie Colony areas were romanticized versions of the Spanish colonial style—red tile roofs, fountains, long walkways, arched doorways, thick adobe walls, dark tile floors. Towering palms and masses of bougainvillea added to the illusion of being in a desert oasis. Another acceptable architectural alternative to Spanish style was an interpretation of the California ranch house—a sprawling, westernized bungalow that offered instant access to the outdoors from all rooms.

After the war, a new style of resort living was defined by the architects practicing in the area. The mid-century era has been termed "modern"—every fifty years or so we seem to purge ourselves of our predecessors' possessions and taste so that we can leave our own imprint. The houses built during the 1940s and 1950s in the desert were "modern" thanks to their intelligent, functional, and well-reasoned design; the willingness of the architects to test advanced techniques and use new products; and the enthusiasm with which their clients accepted these newfangled ideas.

A handful of the houses were crafted by architects who had established international reputations. Some were done by well-known architects based in Los Angeles who had been asked by their clients to do a second house. But the bulk of the modernist architecture in Palm Springs was executed by a handful of men, all of whom settled there in the 1930s and 1940s. They were guided by different gods of modernism—Walter Gropius, Alvar Aalto, Mies van der Rohe, and Le Corbusier—but they all respected the desert environment and learned how to build with it. Their houses remain "modern" because their budgets were often limited, but they still had to resolve complex problems of hot days and cold nights, intense sunlight, and accompanying dryness. Their architecture responded to the desert as well as to the modernism being preached and practiced at the time. They perfected what they prefer to call not "modernism" but "desert architecture."

Many of the projects they designed in the Palm Springs area from the late 1930s to the late 1960s were hugely influential, in part because they were published regularly in *Palm Springs Life*, the *Los Angeles Times Home* magazine, *Arts and Architecture*, *Architectural Record*, *Architectural Digest*, and *House and Garden*. *Life* and *Time* gave design and architecture extensive coverage. Layouts on movie stars' homes were always guaranteed to increase circulation. The magazines showed how new products and materials were being incorporated into kitchens and bathrooms. They ran features on steel-frame houses and aluminum siding in the desert. Readers across the country were left to daydream about a life spent playing golf every day and swimming outdoors on winter evenings. And in a house right on top of the golf course! The pool was a given.

It was a period of unshackling, a turning of backs on the ornately decorative Spanish style of the 1920s and 1930s. Out went the sloping tile roofs, wrought-iron grilles over balconies, arched windows, plaster walls, and gloomy interiors. In came a lightweight frame of steel, floor-to-ceiling glass windows and sliding doors, flat roofs, and thin beams. By the time modernism was in full swing in Palm Springs in the 1960s, there was little interest in building in the Spanish vernacular.

In its own way, golf had an enormous impact on desert architecture. As the recreational sport thrived in the early 1950s, developers needed a way to sell acres of sand dunes in the middle of nowhere as potential golf courses. There was abundant water from underground artesian wells, but visions of rolling fairways and perfect greens were probably hard to grasp, and even tougher to sell. And so a new concept in resort living was born—housing built right around the golf course. When country clubs started thriving in the early 1950s in

18

In its own way, golf had an enormous impact on desert architecture.

Cathedral City, Rancho Mirage, and Indian Wells, lots were offered alongside the fairway. Bob Hope and Bing Crosby bought at Thunderbird Country Club, the first club built with fairway housing, as did Lucille Ball and Desi Arnaz. Gerald Ford also chose Thunderbird following his term as president. Frank Sinatra, after living in a house designed by local architect E. Stewart Williams, moved into Tamarisk Country Club. Dwight and Mamie Eisenhower lived in a Welton Becket–designed house at Eldorado Country Club. Architects had been handed the perfect scenario—an empty desert, a brand-new country club with as many lots squeezed in as feasible, and clients used to having houses professionally built and decorated. As a bonus, it was a brave new era of construction and engineering. The architects could launch the vacation house into the future, and some did.

The desert didn't appeal just to movie stars and the wealthy. Many of the GIs who had been based in Palm Springs during the war returned, drawn by the climate and cheap land. And that in turn attracted a small group of young architects who were breaking away from ponderous traditional building styles. They had absorbed the modernist influence emanating from Europe (via magazines and their own travels) and were eager to test their own modern sensibilities on such an attractive and undeveloped canvas.

Palm Springs offered itself as a blank slate, but it was an extremely beautiful one. To the west rise the protective San Jacinto Mountains, often snow-capped, and always counted on to keep out the smog and clouds drifting over from Los Angeles. To the southwest are the pink Santa Rosa Mountains. The valley floor is pocked with oases dense with date palms. To the east is the yellow and pink of the desert and north are the Little San Bernardino Mountains. The San Andreas Fault runs straight down the middle of the Coachella Valley.

For about thirty years, there was a confluence of talent, wealth, and taste in that secluded Shangri-la, and the proof—the mid-century modern houses and commercial buildings that still stand—is testament to the vision of the architects and their clients. An extraordinary group of individuals landed in Palm Springs at the same time. Their only common denominator was an appreciation for a modern approach to living, but they would leave an architectural legacy that remains unsurpassed in its diversity, originality, and international influence.

The Architectural Roots—1920s and 1930s

Palm Springs took its Spanish colonial persona in the 1920s and 1930s from the founding group of "matriarchs" who ruled village society, owned land, ran profitable businesses, and dictated its architectural style: Pearl McCallum McManus, Nellie Coffman, Ruth Hardy, the White sisters, and Zaddie Bunker. Along with developers and realtors Alvah Hicks, Culver Nichols, and Prescott T. Stevens, they understood the area's potential as a winter resort. All the natural elements were in place: a sheltered mountain location, year-round sun, clean dry air, an unlimited water supply, groves of palm trees, and mineral hot springs.

Before they discovered the Coachella Valley and its natural springs, the only inhabitants had been the Cahuilla Indians, and their stone-and-adobe abodes were hidden away in the Indian Canyons. None of the Spanish conquistadors or missionaries had ventured into the valley, so the Spanish colonial style that was so pervasive in southern California had never taken root. Surveyors looking for a southern route for the Southern Pacific Railway, prospectors, and stagecoach operators in Banning had opened the door to a handful of white settlers in the 1850s. John Guthrie McCallum arrived from San Francisco in 1885 to serve as an Indian agent for the government; he would dig the first irrigation ditch that ran from the White-water River into the village and he incorporated the Palm Valley Land and Water Company. But an eleven-year drought drove him out of business and left many settlers desperate to sell their parcels of land. The permanent population in the 1920s, which numbered about two hundred, was swollen in the winter months by visitors taking the waters at the spas. Few people before the advent of refrigerated air-conditioning stayed through the summer; most escaped to cabins in the local mountains at Idyllwild or to Santa Barbara and San Diego on the coast.

The "matriarchs" set up and served on a design review board (one city code stated that you had to hire an architect to get something built). An aesthetically soothing hybrid of Spanish hacienda, Mission revival, and Italian villa styles was developed for the hotels and shops that were springing up on Palm Canyon Drive and Indian Avenue. El Mirador Hotel, built in 1926 in the north of town, was given a Moorish minaret. Nellie Coffman's Desert Inn sprawled in twenty hacienda-style cottages over thirty lush acres downtown. Ruth Hardy converted a private adobe estate into the Ingleside Inn. The women also made sure that no factories or industrial plants were allowed in the near vicinity. Horseback riding was still the most popular activity, and the horse set settled into the low-key atmosphere and protected desert environment of Smoke Tree Ranch, which had (briefly) served as the Palm Springs terminus for the narrow-gauge railway that connected to Southern Pacific's main line at Seven Palms, seven miles away. Within the four-hundred-acre Smoke Tree Ranch, the city's first private community enclave where street names were painted on rocks and utilities were laid underground, the ranch house bungalow was fully embraced.

The first large wave of settlers started arriving in the 1920s and 1930s. Hollywood was enjoying the public's dependence on movies during the Depression. More than ten movies a year were being filmed in the desert, which provided the perfect stand-in for the Mediterranean or Africa. Al Jolson, King Gillette, Jack Warner, Harold Lloyd, and Darryl Zanuck built Spanish-style estates or ranch houses in Palm Springs. Alan Ladd helped a friend open a hardware store. Business tycoons and their wives arrived by train and car from Ohio, Illinois, British Columbia, Oklahoma, and Texas, leaving their children in boarding schools while they escaped the cold. Prospectors came hoping to tap into any or all of the area's resources: water, oil, land, minerals. Those with tuberculosis, asthma, and arthritis came to take the waters at the spa in town, where natural hot springs and mud baths bubbled on land owned by the Cahuilla Indians, who had been dubbed the Agua Caliente. The rickety cabin over the springs was replaced by a "solid little bath-house," wrote J. Smeaton Chase in 1920. Nellie Coffman opened the Desert Inn Hotel and Sanatorium in 1909.

Thomas O'Donnell added a nine-hole golf course. Pearl McCallum McManus inherited no money from her father but had been left the deeds to his land—some five thousand acres. She turned to local resident Lloyd Wright (who was temporarily estranged from his father) in 1924 to design the Oasis Hotel, an Art Deco concoction with a central tower that later housed Loretta Young's rooms. Former carpenter Alvah F. Hicks arrived from New York in 1913, bought the water company from Judge John McCallum, renamed it the Palm

PALM SPRINGS DESERT MUSEUM / E. STEWART WILLIAMS ARCHIVES

In a 1932 aerial view of the Coachella Valley, "the little village of Palm Springs is etched in the raw desert flood plain," wrote architect Stewart Williams.

Springs Water Company (now the Desert Water Agency), and created some of the village's best developments: Las Palmas, where Spanish colonial–style estates take up entire blocks; and Little Tuscany, where, inspired by a visit to Tuscany, Hicks decreed that only Italianate houses were allowed (a condition that has thankfully expired). Julia Carnell had dispatched Dayton architect Harry Williams by plane to Santa Barbara to check out its popular Spanish colonial–style Plaza shopping center, and he returned with sketches of its tile roofs and ornate wrought-iron grilles and plans for a similar shopping center that would straddle the two main roads in town—Palm Canyon Drive and Indian Avenue. More importantly, the Palm Springs Plaza was built around a parking lot, one of the first uses of interior, off-street parking in southern California.

During World War II, the entire village turned itself over to serving the air force base. A new airstrip was built in 1942. General Patton conducted tank exercises before heading to Sicily and North Africa. El Mirador Hotel, where Marlene Dietrich had played tennis and Amos and Andy had been broadcast for six years, was converted into the Torney General Hospital.

In April 1938, the 910 registered voters of the village elected to incorporate Palm Springs into a city.

The Moderns—the 1940s, 1950s, and 1960s

The town really kicked into cocktail hour in the late 1940s and 1950s when Frank Sinatra, Bob Hope, Bing Crosby, Lucille Ball, Cary Grant, Clark Gable, Jack Warner, Jack Benny, Edgar Bergen, Randolph Scott, the Gabor sisters, William Powell, Mervyn LeRoy, Frank Capra, Red Skelton, William Holden, Harpo Marx, Dinah Shore, Liberace, and Kirk Douglas moved in. Palm Springs was the ideal escape from the film set and the press. At that time, it was a dusty four-hour drive from Los Angeles and inaccessible enough that the only photographers hovering around the stars were employed by the hotels and nightclubs. Directors, screenwriters, set decorators, and fashion designers joined the weekend exodus. Bob and Dolores Hope, who have had places in Palm Springs for fifty years, asked John Lautner to build them a house in 1973 that has since become an architectural beacon. Frank Sinatra, who was also a fifty-year resident and honorary mayor of Cathedral City, celebrated his first million dollars by commissioning a house with a pool shaped like a grand piano.

Until the city's main airport was built in 1965, there was one small airstrip, an office, and a hangar at the end of a dirt road off Indian Avenue. Rita Hayworth in her singing days would fly in when performing locally. Peggy Lee, Louis Armstrong, Nat King Cole, and Bing Crosby appeared at the Chi Chi, which was a few doors down from the Desert Inn. Gambling flourished in neighboring Cathedral City. John F. Kennedy came to town—often. At first he stayed at Frank Sinatra's compound at Tamarisk, and then with Bing Crosby in Thunderbird. Norman Mailer set *The Deer Park* there. French-born industrial designer Raymond Loewy chose Swiss-born architect Albert Frey to design a vacation house. Edgar J. Kaufmann, who had commissioned Fallingwater from Frank Lloyd Wright, asked Richard Neutra, based in Los Angeles, to design his Palm Springs residence. Cary Grant and Walt Disney preferred the low-key ambiance of Smoke Tree Ranch, where the entertainment of choice was an overnight horseback ride into the canyons and a chuck-wagon dinner. The

Racquet Club, founded in 1932 by Charlie Farrell, who would become mayor, and actor Ralph Bellamy, was the social gathering spot for tennis and then dancing at its Bamboo Bar. Albert Frey later added eleven guest cottages clustered around a giant chess set. The Tennis Club, owned by Pearl McCallum McManus, was set on a rocky outcropping against the mountains and featured an oval pool; its clubhouse was designed in 1947 by Los Angeles architects A. Quincy Jones and Paul Williams. John Lautner built the four-unit Desert Hot Springs Motel in 1947. Wurdeman and Becket designed a chic setting on Palm Canyon Drive in 1946 for Bullock's Wilshire. In 1957 William Pereira arrived to create two adjoining stores in lightweight steel for J. W. Robinson's. Air-conditioned office buildings by Clark and Frey, and Williams, Williams, and Williams were turning Palm Canyon Drive into a fashionable stretch for working, shopping, and dining.

By the late 1940s, Spanish anything was considered yawningly old-fashioned and provincial. The Bauhaus teachings of Walter Gropius, the sophisticated elegance of Mies van der Rohe, and the machine-age functionalism of Le Corbusier were revolutionizing architecture, and their work, widely published in magazines, spread their philosophy west. They made modern design seem light, bright, sophisticated, and affordable. Rudolph Schindler and Richard Neutra brought the stripped-down rigors of what was called the International Style from Austria to Los Angeles, where architecture was reaping the benefits of the postwar construction boom. The building technology that was being developed in the Los Angeles basin and the increasing availability of materials had a direct effect on the architects and construction industry in the desert just hours away.

As affluent vacationers from Chicago and points east increased in number, so did the clamor for a modern house that didn't have the bulk or heaviness of the traditional styles they had left behind. They expected the desert to provide something more experimental and rule-breaking. At the same time, the GIs returning after the war needed low-cost housing, plenty of jobs, good schools, and a promise of the good life. The desert had it all.

Schindler and Neutra were already well known when they left their architectural marks in the desert. Wallace Neff, Paul R. Williams, A. Quincy Jones, Wurdeman and Becket, William Pereira, Conrad Buff, Craig Ellwood, and John Lautner had successful practices in Los Angeles. But it was John Porter Clark, Albert Frey, E. Stewart Williams, and William F. Cody who participated in the village's metamorphosis into a city. They arrived in the 1930s and 1940s from Ohio, Iowa, even Switzerland, fortified with visions of a new way of living. Until the 1980s, Clark and Frey and brothers Stewart and Roger Williams worked together—in an ever-changing, interdependent swirl of partnerships and associations—on all of the city's municipal buildings that line Tahquitz Canyon Way: City Hall, the police department, the Civic Center. They collaborated on the Palm Springs Aerial Tramway and Palm Springs High School. Bill Cody, the larger-than-life maverick, excelled at houses, restaurants, hotels, and country clubs. They were instrumental in stamping a modern form onto Palm Springs's banks and libraries, schools and churches, gas stations and offices.

The desert demanded a new way of living and a new way of thinking about how to live. People wanted to be outdoors when they were there—that was the whole point. Days were spent in or around the pool. Winter evenings called for fires. Spring evenings were velvety warm and smooth, the air redolent with fragrant flowers. Twilight was the perfect time for

By the late 1940s, Spanish anything was considered yawningly old-fashioned and provincial.

cocktails served poolside. To help ease the flow of traffic, large sliding glass doors were introduced. At dusk, the walls of glass that enclosed living areas literally vanished, sliding effortlessly open and obliterating the division between indoors and out. Spotlights highlighted the fruit trees and oleander that surrounded azure swimming pools and spas.

The house could be transparent and weightless—let the backdrop of date palms and the snow-capped San Jacinto Mountains to the west and the pinks and yellows of the dunes to the east dominate. Since most houses were used only in winter, when the sun shone lower in the sky, clerestories were added wherever possible to let in extra bands of light. Wall divisions between rooms became fewer and lower. Massive flat-roof overhangs, needed as sun protection, created outside terraces that felt like indoor spaces; some terraces were furnished as such, with rugs and chandeliers.

After some experimentation, the architects learned how to adapt to the climate and its restrictions. In the desert, they could experiment with rocks and stone, steel and concrete. They usually didn't make much money designing vacation houses, but a tight budget forced them to rethink how the house could function in a truly "modern" way within its environment.

Their credos became a common-sense response to building in the desert: Don't use wood on exteriors (unless you're Stewart Williams) since it expands, contracts, and disintegrates rapidly. Avoid stucco and plaster—they crack easily. Use only steel, concrete, stone, glass. Build the house low on the ground and let it conform to the landscape. Make the outdoors as much a part of the indoors as possible. Keep ornamentation to a minimum or, rather, incorporate it into the house through its materials—granite boulders, volcanic rock, riverbed stones, textured concrete, contrasting woods, baked aluminum, and exposed steel. Water became a much-used element indoors and out, a natural coolant that was introduced as swimming pools, fountains, waterfalls, ponds, and water channels.

Golf drove the tourist boom. In 1951 one-time professional golfer Johnny Dawson, Frank Bogert (former manager of El Mirador and future mayor of Palm Springs), and a group of investors took over the 182-acre Thunderbird Dude Ranch in Rancho Mirage and opened the first eighteen-hole golf course/residential development. The $7,000 fee to join Thunderbird Country Club was split between a $2,000 homesite and the $5,000 club membership. Within a year, half of the eighty-seven lots had been sold. Bing Crosby, Jimmy Van Heusen, and Phil Harris and wife Alice Faye were among its original members. The chairman of Ford named his new sports car model after the club. When Dwight Eisenhower first visited Palm Springs in 1954 he played a round of golf at Thunderbird, and the city's image as an elite winter playground was permanently fixed in the public's conscience. The elegant La Quinta Hotel, a Spanish colonial revival built in 1929, was purchased by Dawson along with a thousand adjacent acres, and in 1958 La Quinta Country Club, now the official home of the PGA West, opened. Tamarisk, where Ben Hogan was the pro, opened in 1952, followed by Indian Wells in 1958 and Eldorado in 1959. All the while, Bill Cody, practitioner of some of the most elegantly restrained architecture in the desert, was honing his designs for clubhouses and private fairway housing, first at Thunderbird, then at Tamarisk, and finally at the Taj Mahal of golf—the Eldorado Country Club in Indian Wells.

They usually didn't make much money designing vacation houses, but a tight budget forced them to rethink how the house could function in a truly "modern" way within its environment.

Decline and Rebound—the 1970s on

Twenty years after reigning as the height of fashionable living, modernism died its own slow death. By the 1970s it seemed dated and severe, stuck in the hopelessly suburban fifties. Wealth and prosperity demanded a brasher, more overt kind of decorative display. The next generation insisted on its own style.

In the early 1960s George Alexander and his son Robert started developing huge housing tracts behind the Riviera Hotel and next to Little Tuscany. The majority of their tract houses were designed by architects Palmer and Krisel as a mass-market take on modernism. They filled cul-de-sacs and lanes with rows of sprawling, A-frame bungalows with asymmetrical butterfly roofs, which made the houses look larger and more dramatic, and offered high ceilings and plenty of shaded parking. Palm Springs would be the testing ground for Dick Weis's concept for cooperative condominium living, another factor that would contribute to denser living quarters and a corresponding population increase. By the mid-1970s the permanent population, which now included many year-round residents thanks to air-conditioning, had reached twenty-five thousand; during the "season" that figure would triple to include part-time residents and visitors.

One reaction to all that sober modernism was a refreshing layer of kitsch—mirrored front doors, statues of peeing cupids surrounding colonnaded pools, shiny white and blue faux Greek villas, Alpine-style chalets, acres of green and orange shag, Rolls-Royce golf carts—that started to rear its impudent head. Decorators went wild with yellow and red. A house custom designed by Palmer and Krisel for developer Bob Alexander in 1962, where Elvis and Priscilla Presley honeymooned, has been turned into an homage to Elvis; Liberace's villa still has a chandelier hanging out in the front lawn. Happily, the 1970s also produced the serpentine Charthouse restaurant by Ken Kellogg, and John Lautner's turtleback residence for Dolores and Bob Hope.

In the mid-1960s seven local architects, Bill Cody and Stewart Williams among them, had been asked by the city to study how to restructure downtown, which had become clogged with traffic and unmanageable at rush hour. The report they presented to the city council for a new convention center, hotel, museum, and shopping center was "filed for reference." The architects were at the pinnacle of their careers, but they gradually withdrew from taking on public projects.

Twenty years of population and construction booms had left Palm Springs exhausted and depleted. The property tax reductions of Proposition 13 didn't help the city's finances. A building moratorium was declared and the mid-1970s became a period of no growth. Developers started eyeing the outlying communities of Rancho Mirage, Palm Desert, and Indian Wells, which offered the land and building opportunities that Palm Springs no longer could. As Palm Springs leaked money and residents fled, all attempts at maintaining a design review board that oversaw a cohesive city plan were cast aside. Several blocks downtown that had contained the Desert Inn and Bullocks were torn down and replaced with malls or parking lots. Architects were no longer consulted on review board decisions. The city limited its design control to street lamps and sidewalk benches. Postmodernism, with its pastel pink and green palette and stylized pyramids and columns, was welcomed as the savior of the dowdy modern buildings the city felt it was saddled with. And Spanish anything, watered down in the 1980s to a generic Mediterranean look, was back, this time viewed as the perfect ornamental antidote to the rather unpopular 1940s and 1950s modernist schools and commercial buildings that had mushroomed downtown.

By 1968, when Arthur Elrod, the town's most famous interior decorator, asked John Lautner for "the house you think I should have" on the eastern end of Palm Springs, Rancho Mirage and Palm Desert were positioning themselves as more updated alternatives. Their brand-new houses were bigger, designed in a more consumer-friendly Mediterranean style, and offered better amenities. As Palm Springs stagnated, young families and the wealthy moved east into gated communities and country clubs. Backed up against the mountains, Palm Springs lacked the open space needed to develop its own competitive golf courses and country clubs. The town was starting to look outmoded and tired.

Palm Springs lay dormant and undisturbed for another twenty years until the mid-1990s, when interest in mid-century modern architecture and design started to swell. The 1950s were reevaluated as a period that produced an explosion of ideas and purity of design that has not been matched since. Palm Springs was nudged awake by location scouts and magazine crews from Los Angeles, New York, France, and Germany.

The majority of the following gems of mid-century modern architecture were stumbled upon in their original condition, some still occupied by their original owners. The impact that these architects and homeowners had on the desert oasis between the 1940s and the 1960s is immeasurable. The town's current revival as a "hot" hot spot and the worldwide acclaim being accorded its architecture is gratifying to those who thought their work had gone undiscovered or, worse, ignored. Now it has come full circle, for some in their own lifetime.

PALM SPRINGS MODERN

John Porter Clark House, 1939

John Porter Clark, Architect

By the age of seventeen John Porter Clark had already built an adobe house for his sister in Beaumont. Born in Iowa in 1905 but raised in southern California, Clark had studied architecture at Cornell and was designing eclectic Spanish/Italian Renaissance estates in Pasadena with Marston Van Pelt and Maybury when he was invited out to Palm Springs in 1932 by Culver and Sally Nichols to help develop the town. "It was the bottom of the Depression, and there was more construction work in the desert than in Los Angeles," he recalled in a 1986 interview. Clark became the first licensed architect to be registered in Palm Springs.

The house he built for himself in 1939, when he was still a bachelor, was a simple box on stilts, a radical departure from the Spanish style prevalent in the village at the time. Clark's house was elevated above the ground "primarily so I could retain a view of the mountains over the treetops," he explained. "But of course the trees grew and blocked the view." The stilts served another, more practical purpose — they created a space under the house for parking automobiles, which were becoming a crucial part of the American household, particularly on the West Coast. "I was developing designs more along the style of the ranch house — trying to clean up the old style and make houses more compatible with automobiles." The area underneath the upper living room is divided into a carport on the more exposed side and a sheltered patio on the inner, more protected side. The structure consists of angular wood beams and framework painted "Golden Gate Bridge red," corrugated metal facing, pipe railing, and pipe supports set into prestressed concrete.

Clark's residence expands on the concepts of the Aluminaire House, a low-cost light-steel-and-aluminum project created by Albert Frey and A. Lawrence Kocher for the Architectural League of New York's 1931 exhibition. It was one of the few American houses included in Philip Johnson and Henry-Russell Hitchcock's influential show on International Style modern architecture at the Museum of Modern Art in 1932. The Zurich-born Frey, who had been heavily influenced by the innovative work of Le Corbusier, arrived in Palm Springs a year after Clark, and they started working together from 1935 to 1937. "We had common goals and shared a love for the desert environment," Clark said. Frey went back to New York for two years to assist on the Museum of Modern Art but returned to the desert in 1939 and resumed his partnership with Clark, which would continue for almost twenty years, producing some of the most influential architecture in Palm Springs. The two men were very similar in their ascetic taste — both seemed excited more by a project's engineering challenges than its design. Frey's idea of a house on stilts provided Clark with the solution of how to integrate the house and the garage.

Before construction started, Clark and Frey planted a ten-foot pole on the property and spent a year charting the angles of the sun. (That chart would prove extremely useful to them in gauging how

The bachelor house that Clark built in 1939 was a single-story structure raised on stilts—one of the first houses to bring modern design
concepts to Palm Springs. "International Style is an unfortunate and
misused term that doesn't describe anything except the elimination of
ornamentation," he said.
Overleaf: Clark, who read Maya hieroglyphics, based the Maya-style
fountain in the circular motor court on one he had designed for the
College of the Desert. The living area was raised on stilts to allow
parking for the increasingly ubiquitous automobile. Stairs at back
lead up to the kitchen.

to site future projects.) Corrugated iron instead of wood was used to deal with the effects of extreme heating and cooling. Little insulation was needed since electricity was cheap. An evaporative cooling system was installed, the most efficient means of cooling a house prior to the arrival of air-conditioning. To add much-needed softness against the desert landscape, as well as protection against high winds, Clark supplemented rows of tamarisks with elms, palm trees, bamboo, oleander, and hibiscus. In the center of the motor court is a Mayan-inspired fountain, graceful and modern. The original irrigation channel, fed by the Whitewater River, still waters the property once a week.

In 1946, after the Clarks' first son was born, they added a separate bedroom wing on the other side from the entry, where each room has its own hotel-like entrance. "At the time we built the bedrooms, the second floor was converted into a dining room/kitchen/living room," said Clark. "Having a separate building was very convenient. We could park the children there and we had a sound box, so that if we heard them crying we could tell them to go back to sleep without having to go downstairs. It created a privacy, which we liked." "The architectural style is very much like J. P.'s personality — no-nonsense pragmatism," says his younger son, Stanley, who returned to live in his childhood home with his wife and their daughters in 1991, a year after his father died. "His was not an emotional, romantic architecture — he was more interested in materials and in progressive design."

Clark had been offered his plot of land by Prescott T. Stevens, a Colorado cattleman who in 1920 constructed the fabled El Mirador Hotel on his land holdings in the northern part of town. Stevens lost control of the hotel in 1932 but his daughter Sally, who married realtor Culver Nichols, retained the land behind it — the village's first eighteen-hole golf course lined with tamarisk trees that marked the fairways. Sally Stevens sold the lot next to Clark's to Albert Frey, and a third lot to architect E. Stewart Williams, who arrived in the mid-1940s. In 1938 the village incorporated itself into the city of Palm Springs, and Clark and then Frey became the city's "social" architects, responsible for generating a wide spectrum of public buildings that always came in on time and on budget. For the first six months of World War II, Clark worked as the resident architect during the conversion of El Mirador Hotel into the Torney General Hospital; he then joined the Army Corps of Engineers as an architect.

Preceding pages: A giant elm shades the inner court-yard. The sheltered patio under the house serves as an outdoor living room.

Right: Simplicity of line and detail are evident at the entrance door. Clark used corrugated metal, since it cooled rapidly, and the same pecky cypress paneling that was used in Raymond Loewy's house.

Residential design, however, was not an area he wanted to explore — Clark did few private houses in Palm Springs, but one of his best was for Santa Barbara art collector Wright Ludington. He preferred entering the public realm. "Engineering was his forte," says son Stanley. "Bridges, roads. He enjoyed exploring how a project best fit its landscape." Clark was a charter member of the city's planning commission, appointed by its first mayor, Philip Boyd. Under the commission's guidance, official buildings moved away from the adobe Spanish style and took on a strictly modernist shape. Clark and Frey's City Hall, practically all the schools in the unified school district, and the police department each have a distinctive, unified postwar style that is efficient, functional, of low maintenance, and was inexpensive to build. Clark designed the city's first school, Nellie Coffman Junior High, and the College of the Desert. He did the preliminary set of drawings for engineer Francis Crocker, who dreamed of a cable car that would transport visitors to the top of the mountains. After the war, Clark became the project architect of the Palm Springs Aerial Tramway (1949–63), the cable car that travels in fourteen minutes from the desert floor over five enormous pylons on the 8,500-foot ascent to the snow and pine trees of Mount San Jacinto. It was a local triumph of design, engineering, and collaboration: Clark, Frey, and their third partner, Robson C. Chambers, based the design for the valley station on a New England covered bridge; Stewart and Roger Williams contributed an elegant Alpine-style mountain station and restaurant.

"J. P.'s design philosophy was based on function more than form," says Stanley Clark. "When he was in the army, he would do whatever the job required. He enjoyed that discipline. His palette was influenced by the army — jeep greens, tank browns, very subtle blends of beiges and desert colors. He thought architecture was the function of a group, not just one person, and that it represented a movement of a culture. He felt that his own opinion wasn't primary. He was self-effacing to a fault." •

"His palette was influenced by the army—jeep greens, tank browns, very subtle blends of beiges and desert colors."

Above: The rectangular pool, which wasn't added until 1982, faces the San Jacinto Mountains. "Before the pool was put in, we ran through sprinklers in the summer," says Clark's younger son, Stanley.

Left: Clark echoed the pattern of the staircase in the louvered runner that connects the lower-level overhang to the second-story roof.

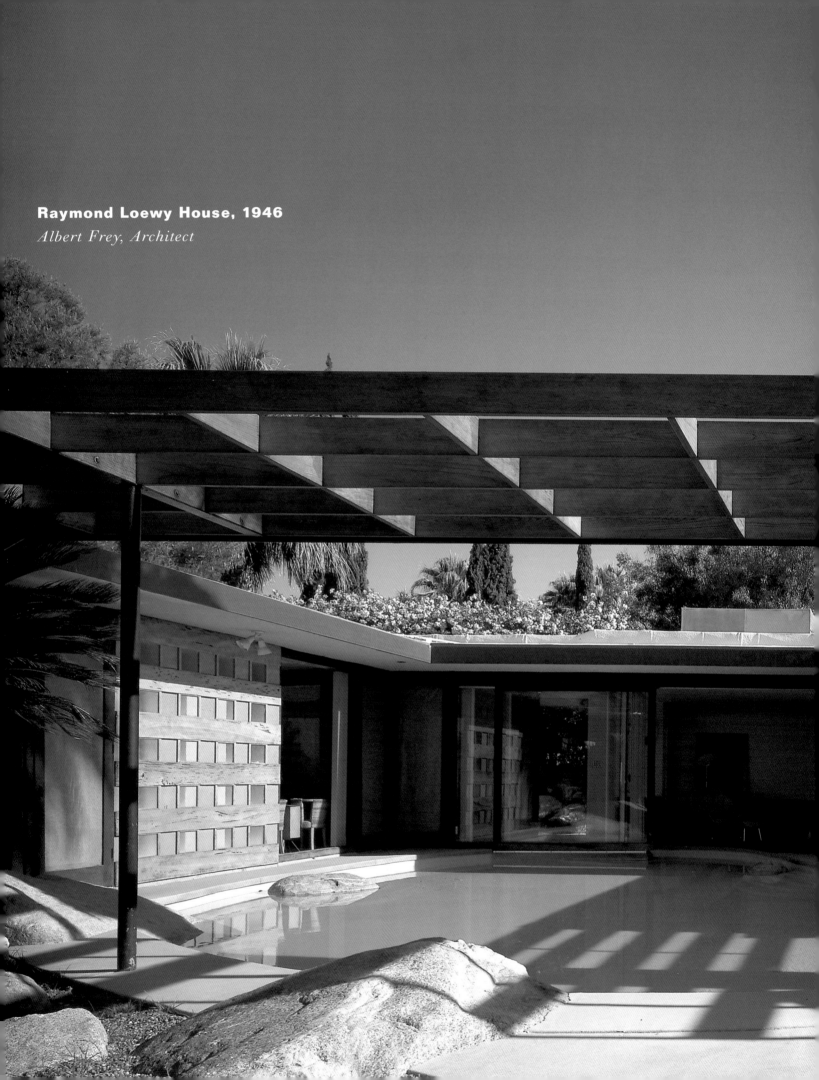

Raymond Loewy House, 1946

Albert Frey, Architect

In the winter of 1945 Raymond Loewy visited and fell in love with Palm Springs. "I felt very happy, and I walked a great deal through the desert at the foot of Mount San Jacinto. On one of these treks, I found an interesting spot on the side of a low hill. It was a maze of granite boulders, some of gigantic dimensions, all pale gray in color, part of a prehistoric glacier. I thought it would be a perfect site for a small desert retreat," wrote Loewy in his 1950 autobiography, *Never Leave Well Enough Alone*.

"Loewy used to stay at the Racquet Club," recalls Albert Frey, who had designed the club's cottages and knew its owners, Charlie Farrell and Ralph Bellamy. "One day he came into the office and said, 'I want to build a house here.'" Loewy would have preferred to have bought land higher up in Little Tuscany, but association rules there permitted only "Italian" design and he would not have been allowed to build the modern house he wanted. So he bought two acres on a lower, sloping lot surrounded by citrus, banana, and palm trees and cactus and drew up some sketches. "A lot of the rocks had been pushed onto the property when they were building the roads," says Frey, "so we left most of them. He wanted to use them and they made the project more interesting."

The French-born Loewy (1893–1986) was establishing a worldwide reputation as the most prominent and prolific of a new breed: the industrial designer. His name was attached to the more readily identifiable products of the era — Coldspot and Frigidaire refrigerators, the Greyhound bus, Studebaker cars, logos for Shell and Exxon, new packaging for Lucky Strike, and the iconic Coca-Cola bottle. He had homes in Mexico, St. Tropez, and Long Island. As the salesman who was convincing corporate America to share his vision of a streamlined future, Loewy recognized a power center when he saw one, and in winter Palm Springs qualified as red hot. When President Kennedy flew into town in 1963, Loewy came away from the airport "unimpressed by the gaudy red exterior markings and what seemed to me the amateurish graphics of Air Force One." To this day Air Force One bears Loewy's redesigned aquamarine typography.

In Loewy's house, four well-veined boulders delineated the free-form pool, which was kept heated at eighty degrees. The pool, which Frey calls "pure Loewy," didn't stop outside, however; it flowed past the partially submerged boulders, under the thirty-foot-long sliding doors, right into the living room, ending at a carpet three feet from the front door. The position of the pool would prove problematic, especially during parties. Someone would invariably fall in. Loewy recounted that at the housewarming party, actor and neighbor William Powell accidentally fell in fully clothed. To save him from embarrassment, Tony Martin followed suit. Loewy, ever the gracious host, elected to join them.

"It was an interesting collaboration with Loewy because he had wonderfully inventive ideas," says Frey. Loewy insisted on using pecky cypress (a worm-eaten pickled wood that reminded him of the desert) for the interior walls and outside trim for the house and trellis. The trapezoidal redwood

The position of the pool would prove problematic, especially during parties. Someone would invariably fall in.

A trapezoidal redwood trellis wraps around the free-form pool, connecting the master bedroom to the semicircular dining room at left. "I wanted to own a small isolated house in the desert," Raymond Loewy said. "Due to its low profile, to its color matching the rocks and sand, the house blends with the desert and is hardly visible."

Overleaf: After he married, Loewy enclosed the open solarium and turned it into a dining room. He hung an amoeba-shaped stone slab from the Salton Sea over the living room fireplace.

Preceding pages: The pool flows under sliding doors to within three feet of the front door. Albert Frey added glass blocks and shelves inside the bathroom and master bedroom so that Loewy's collection of glass objects would glow at night.

Right: A pane of corrugated glass was the only interruption of the view south when the house was built. Bottles filled with pink-colored water were placed around the pool.

JULIUS SHULMAN

trellis angled from the master bedroom around the pool to the kitchen and acted as a frame for the panoramic view. The trellis widened into a shelter for an outdoor terrace that Loewy called a "solarium." A sheet of corrugated glass, protection against the high winds, ran between two poles supporting the trellis and was the only man-made interruption on the horizon.

Frey placed a grid of pecky cypress outside the master bedroom and bathroom windows and built glass blocks and shelves inside so that Loewy's collection of pots and vases could be displayed glowingly at night. Around the pool were glass bottles from Mexico filled with pink-colored water.

Loewy despised "bad modern" design, especially furniture, and the home's furnishings were kept deliberately simple and easy to maintain. Mounted on walls in and around the house were amoebic stone slabs that he brought back from the Salton Sea nearby. "Everything — including the furniture — is sand colored, the exterior as well. When the lights are off, the pool alone can be illuminated by a powerful submerged lamp, and the scene resembles a blue lagoon in a desert oasis," he wrote.

Loewy called his Palm Springs house Tierra Caliente (he would give the same name to his villa in Tetelpan, Mexico) and he spent several weeks there each winter, at first on his own and then with his wife and their daughter. He drew up the preliminary designs for the Avanti at the house in 1961.

After Loewy married in 1948 he enclosed the solarium as a dining area and added a separate bedroom and a studio. "When the house is kept in darkness, but for a log fire and candles, the sight is sheer beauty. A small fountain adds its frail tone to the silence of this oasis. In the distance, we hear the coyotes. Viola is near me; R. L. is happy." •

Loewy had insisted on using pecky cypress for the grid
around the bedroom and bathroom windows. "What I liked
most was the subtlety of the desert coloring, the scents and
the sounds; subdued, restrained, as if nature had blended
everything into a delightful understatement," Loewy wrote.

Edgar J. Kaufmann House, 1946

Richard Neutra, Architect

Richard Neutra had designed a house in Palm Springs before — the 1937 Grace Lewis Miller residence — but in 1946 he would return to build one of his greatest works, the Edgar J. Kaufmann House. Kaufmann, the Pittsburgh department-store magnate, was no stranger to collecting houses and architects. His other house, the seminal Fallingwater, was a country retreat in Pennsylvania created for him in 1935 by Frank Lloyd Wright, and it has become one of the most celebrated and photographed houses in the world. Kaufmann's son had lobbied hard for Wright to be hired for the desert house, too, but Kaufmann Sr. had not been impressed by Taliesin West, the architect's own organic desert experiment in Arizona, and he wanted someone he thought could better capture the Palm Springs lifestyle.

The site in the north of town was not entirely hospitable — on a slope close to the mountains and surrounded by the granite boulders common to the area's alluvial fan. But the 200-by-300-foot lot size and views of the valley and mountains were unbeatable, and Albert Frey had just completed a neighboring house for industrial designer Raymond Loewy. "Modernism seemed drawn to this part of town because the lots were bigger," says the home's current owner, Brent Harris.

Neutra's much documented response to the site was to build "a machine in the garden, juxtaposing a foreign, man-made construct onto a wild, unrefined natural setting." He didn't try to make the house blend into the landscape but instead chose to create geometric quadrants that thrust the rooms out into the landscape in a pinwheel design, like a "ship in the desert."

Neutra was building a house that would be used essentially one month of the year, in January, when Edgar and Liliane Kaufmann would arrive with entourage in tow. Temperatures can reach the nineties during the day and drop to the thirties at night, and a critical component was the invisible heating system. Radiant heat was installed everywhere — walls, ceilings, and floors. The terrace floors outside the living areas and around the pool were heated specifically to draw people out on winter evenings and make the terraces become part of the house. Neutra had also dreamed up a radiant cooling system, but it was never installed. Kaufmann overrode the idea of cooling concrete slabs by running water through them.

The 3,200-square-foot house was an intense collaboration between the two men, who communicated daily via teletype and telegraph. Every detail was analyzed to render the structure as finely crafted and transparent as possible. Kaufmann flew in the stonemasons who had worked on Fallingwater to erect the walls and chimney of Utah buff quartzite sandstone. Cork used in Fallingwater's showers showed up again for the kitchen's countertops and floor and inside showers. One-inch-thick plaster walls were hand-polished with a mica finish. A breezeway protected by adjustable aluminum shutters created an outdoor dining area between the living room and the separate guest rooms. In

The steel and glass Kaufmann House was a sophisticated tour de force that combined technical wizardry in lighting and heating systems with a geometric design that erased the barriers between indoor and outdoor living. The entrance has a low wall of Utah buff quartzite sandstone. Boulders around the property were interspersed with indigenous cactus and shrubs.

Above: Neutra eliminated the corner frames in the master bedroom where the sliding doors meet. During a five-year restoration, multiple layers of paint were stripped from the crimped galvanized sheet-metal fascia, which was given its former aluminum paint finish.

Right: In the interior courtyard quadrant, aluminum louvers protect the breezeway that connects the living area to the guest suites.

Far right: The entranceway is defined by a wall of Utah buff sandstone, set with mortarless joints in an ashlar pattern, and a ceiling of Douglas fir.

"It's very quiet and Zen-like, not like the 'martini modernism' that sprang up here five years later."

the living room and master bedroom, Neutra eliminated the corner frame where the sliding glass doors met; he wanted a seamless passage between the interior and exterior. He evaded the city's restriction on second stories by building what he called a "gloriette" — an open belvedere on the flat roof that was shielded from the elements by adjustable louvered aluminum shutters. Wood floors, a gas fireplace, dumbwaiter, wet bar, and intercom system turned the gloriette into a fully equipped outdoor living room with stunning views.

Water was introduced in a narrow channel, filled with water lilies, that ran the length of the breeze-way in the courtyard quadrant between the living room and guest rooms. The rectangular pool was pushed right up to the house, a few steps from the master bedroom, and was designed with no diving board; it too became a geometric part of the sculptural whole. The lawn planted around the pool was clipped low to imitate a carpet. Neutra designed birch built-in sofa and bed platforms, desks, cabinets, and some of the tables, but the Kaufmanns brought in their own sofa and added reds and yellows to the color scheme. The furniture — Eames chairs, Van Keppel–Green outdoor chaises — was low to the ground and made sitting close to the heated floor an enveloping, luxurious experience.

The Kaufmanns enjoyed the house, which cost $350,000 to complete, from 1947 to 1949. Liliane Kaufmann, who posed by the pool in Julius Shulman's famous twilight photograph, passed away in 1950. Edgar Kaufmann Sr. spent more time in Palm Springs and died at the house in April 1955. Thanks largely to Shulman's widely published photographs, the cubist structure became world renowned, but it sat vacant for eight years and went through three owners and many alterations until Beth and Brent Harris began an intense restoration in 1993. "It's one of the great modern glass houses — it predates Mies's Farnsworth House and Philip Johnson's Glass House," says Beth Harris, who is completing her Ph.D. in architectural history at UCLA. "It's very quiet and Zen-like, not like the 'martini modernism' that sprang up here five years later."

The Harrises chose to take the house back to that twilight moment in Shulman's shot. Using the house as the visual blueprint, Shulman's extensive photographs, and the correspondence and archival drawings at UCLA and Columbia as their guides, they and Santa Monica architects Leo Marmol and Ron Radziner embarked on a three-year archaeological dig. The goal was to clean and repair parts as much as possible or match the original materials.

Right: Water played an important role in softening the design and providing a connection to nature. A lily pond runs the length of the breezeway, which looks into the dining area and living room.

Overleaf: The dining room has Eames chairs and a rug by Raymond Loewy. Neutra brought the clipped lawn close to the house to resemble a carpet. Polished concrete floors with radiant heat extend out to the patios. Low-lying chaises add to the enveloping aura of luxury and comfort.

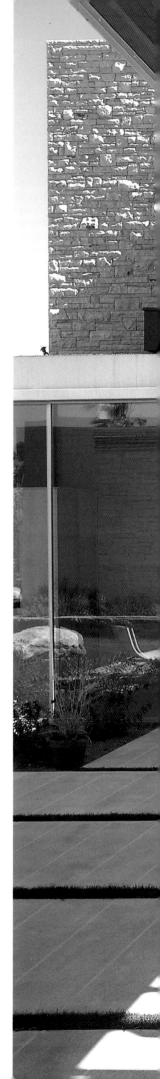

Some problematic areas, especially where the flat roof joined the fireplace, had to be reframed after years of leaks. They returned to the same seam of Utah buff at the quarry to restore the stone wall and chimneys; they found the company in Pasadena that still had the drawings for the metal light fixtures; the machine needed to make the crimped sheet-metal fascia for the boxed facing turned up in a back room in Kansas City. Surrounding lots were reacquired and the landscaping restored with plantings of cactus, ocotillo, oleander, and palo verde trees.

Palm Springs recently designated the house a Class I Historic Site, the first such designation given to a modern, non-Spanish residence in the city. •

Preceding pages: The second-story "gloriette," which functions as an outdoor living area, is a sum of many complex parts: horizontal bands of Douglas fir; vertical louvered shutters that act as protection against high winds and allow for a manipulation of light and shadows; sandstone chimney. An intercom and dumbwaiter connected it to the kitchen below.

Above: The kitchen floor and counter surfaces are of Portuguese cork tiles. "The materials are intrinsically beautiful and not characteristic of Neutra's other work," says owner Brent Harris. "Despite all the changes by previous residents, there was no part of the house that wasn't great, and it struck us as unlikely that we could improve on the original rich palette."

Above: Julius Shulman's 1947 twilight shot of the house has become a modern icon of architectural photography, even though Neutra wanted him to concentrate on documenting the interiors. Shulman grabbed his camera anyway, ran outside and asked Liliane Kaufmann to block out the glare of the pool light while he took three separate exposures over forty-five minutes.

William and Clara Burgess House, 1945–60

William Burgess, Designer

On a steep hillside above Tahquitz Canyon, a private road dug by prison laborers leads to a lush oasis overflowing with palm trees and bougainvillea. After World War II, Bill and Clara Burgess discovered the road, bought a lot, and started building a modest weekend cabin. Bill Burgess had a level shelf blasted out of the side of the mountain and hired Olav Engum, a Norwegian who would spend the next fifteen years digging into the granite with a pneumatic jackhammer, sculpting the mountainside into a weekend retreat. For the first ten years, the couple had to climb fifty stone steps from the road to get to their cabin. Gradually, Engum built up a high retaining wall, using fill to form a level patio, and then a level parking area near the entrance.

Bill Burgess, who used Philip Johnson's Glass House in Connecticut as his inspiration, wanted the cabin to consist entirely of glass and mirrored surfaces so that the walls would seem to disappear and the mountains would be reflected. As the designer and contractor, he could imbue his home with fun-house illusions and sleight-of-hand visual tricks. The modest flat-roof cabana snaked against the hillside and around gray granite boulders streaked with iron and manganese. It had simple eight-foot steel-framed modules for a bedroom, the bathroom, kitchen, and living room facing a pool. The dining area was outside around a sunken pit. Twin bunk beds behind sliding mirrored doors in the living room were for the couple's two daughters.

Burgess set about embellishing the ambience of a desert oasis. The only plantings on the property are palm trees that had to be brought in by crane and masses of red bougainvillea that spill down the hillside (the house is playfully called Bougain Villa). "Clara wanted fruit trees and roses. I wanted an oasis effect — palm trees and bougainvillea," he says. "So we bought a lower lot across the street and planted a rose garden and an orchard there; now we have grapefruit, tangerines, lemons, and limes." Water flows everywhere. Pumps in the swimming pool circulate the water for three waterfalls that cascade behind the house. Two koi ponds are connected by a tunnel to allow the fish to escape raccoons. The master bathroom overlooks water trickling down rocks into a pond filled with volunteer plants.

About twenty years ago the couple decided to sell their house in Pasadena and move permanently to Palm Springs. "When we came here full time, we blasted another twenty feet into the mountain to add a guest room and another bathroom," Bill Burgess says. A massive piece of granite was left as the divider between the bed and bath areas. Water drips down a pipe in the rock into an interior pool. The house now covers about three thousand square feet, with another twenty-five hundred square feet of roof overhang.

It took fifteen years of blasting and jackhammering by Olav Engum to turn an arid mountainside into a lush desert setting for William and Clara Burgess. Bougainvillea cascades down the retaining walls, and palm trees shelter the modest residence.

Preceding pages: Bill Burgess initially stretched canvas shades over the gardening shed and parking area to protect their cars, then repeated the shades around the property at vantage points.

Above: Since the house is composed mostly of glass and mirrored surfaces, decoration is provided by giant urns and pots placed outside.

*Water drips down a granite rock into a pool in the mirrored guest
addition, which neighbor/architect Albert Frey helped design.
The bed and stool are covered with Jack Lenor Larsen's mirrored
Magnum fabric, which the couple also used on the living room sofa.*

With the exception of walnut paneling and bookshelves in parts of the living room, hallway, and the bedrooms, the house is entirely of glass and mirrors. The Burgesses collected modern furniture — by Warren Platner, Charles and Ray Eames, Isamu Noguchi, Eero Saarinen — but there were no surfaces for hanging art so Burgess turned to Moorish-style hanging lanterns and pots as the visual ornamentation. "All the decoration had to be standing or hanging," he says. "The art is three-dimensional here." From the entrance gates, past the pool and into the house, pots stand everywhere and lanterns droop over low conversation areas. The pots and lamps were purchased on the couple's travels to Greece, Spain, the Middle East, even Santa Fe. A Mexican pot came from the window of Bergdorf Goodman's; another was made by the art department head at Skidmore College; others were gifts.

The arched canvas shades that hover over the property are another graceful feature. Burgess first designed two umbrella shades to shelter the couple's cars. A shed for gardening supplies was given the same shade, then two more were added for extra cars. Burgess continued placing shades around the grounds, using the palm trees at the entry gates as cantilevers instead of posts and repeating shades over conversation pits that are scattered at vantage points.

Behind the garage, and practically invisible, is a mirrored pavilion, a separate guest house that Burgess asked his neighbor Albert Frey to help plan. It has become part of the property's vanishing act, a magical mix of mirrors, giant rocks, and water. The couple brought in part of their collection of glass vases and bottles and found a Jack Lenor Larsen mirrored fabric for the bedspread, similar to the fabric on their bed and the living room sofa, thus further uniting the guest house to the main house. •

70

The atmosphere of a desert oasis is embellished by Moroccan lanterns that hang over low conversation pits, and by pots from the Mediterranean and Mexico that frame views of the valley.

…the property's vanishing act, a magical mix of mirrors, giant rocks, and water.

Frank Sinatra House, 1946

E. Stewart Williams, Architect

"It was the first house we did," recalled the late Roger Williams in a 1986 interview. "Frank came into the office in June or July 1946 and told us the main criteria was that he be moved in by Christmas. That allowed three months to come up with the design and three months for construction." Sinatra had just made his first million and he'd promised himself he'd commission something big—a Georgian mansion to be precise, with a red brick facade, columns, and stone balustrades. "I told Frank we'd do that drawing for him but that Stewart would lay out something low-lying in stone and wood that might fit better, and we'd let him decide," said Roger Williams. To the brothers' relief, Sinatra agreed with their desert-appropriate plan. "I'm so glad," said Roger Williams. "We'd have been ruined if we'd been forced to build Georgian in the desert."

Sinatra was married to Nancy at the time, and one of the bedrooms was designed with built-in bunk beds for their children. But they started divorce proceedings in 1950 and he would spend the bulk of his time at the house with his second wife, Ava Gardner. The actress reminisced about their parties and fights there in her 1990 autobiography, *Ava: My Story*: "Maybe it's the air, maybe it's the altitude, maybe it's just the place's goddamn karma, but Frank's establishment in Palm Springs, the only house we really could ever call our own, has seen some pretty amazing occurrences. It was the site of probably the most spectacular fight of our young married life, and honey, don't think I don't know that's really saying something. And even before that it provided me with a chance to spend some time with the most reclusive of Hollywood legends, Greta Garbo."

"It was the site of probably the most spectacular fight of our young married life, and honey, don't think I don't know that's really saying something." – *Ava Gardner*

A circular motor court leads to the garage and the original entrance of Frank Sinatra's first house in Palm Springs, which was called Twin Palms for the two tall palm trees that tower over the property.

Above and right: In a recent renovation, the raised flagstone dining platform in a corner of the living room was removed. Glass doors now form the main point of entry from the front gates at the end of the walkway. Owner Marc Sanders extended the wall of Arizona flagstone into the living room and restored the redwood tongue-and-groove ceiling.

Pages 76–77: At noon, the sun casts shadows in the form of piano keys through the walkway openings. Sinatra asked architect Stewart Williams for a heated pool in the shape of a grand piano. "It was his first house and my first," says Williams, "and it's a little clunky."

JULIUS SHULMAN

JULIUS SHULMAN

JULIUS SHULMAN

JULIUS SHULMAN

Top: The raised platform in the living room once held a round dining table.

Bottom: The house now has such modern pieces as a Florence Knoll sofa and a Robsjohn-Gibbings Cloud table.

Left: Sinatra had the living room equipped with custom recording and sound equipment and brought in a Beverly Hills decorator to furnish the interiors.

Preceding pages: The exterior was sheathed in redwood that deteriorated after Sinatra sold the house. Legend has it that he would hoist a flag at sunset to let neighbors know it was "'tini time."

81

The site chosen in the northern part of town was called Twin Palms for the two tall palm trees that still hold sway over the center of the property. Stewart Williams positioned the house so that the master bedroom had views to the San Jacinto Mountains and the living room looked down to the San Gorgonio Pass. He acquiesced to Sinatra's desire for a heated swimming pool shaped like a grand piano, which cost $8,500 to build at the time, and placed a walkway alongside the pool. At high noon the sun casts a shadow in the form of piano keys through the large square openings in the walkway covering. Sinatra installed enough sound and recording equipment in the living room to necessitate a tall radio antenna that protrudes from the chimney to this day. It was "the first shed-roof house in the desert," says Stewart Williams, who used redwood for the exteriors and interiors, Arizona flagstone for the chimneys, flagstone paving around the pool and cabanas, and copper plumbing throughout. The dining area was located on a raised flagstone platform in a corner of the living room. A single motorized sliding glass door opened the entire living area to the pool. Although Stewart Williams designed many of the built-ins, Sinatra brought in his own Beverly Hills decorator to furnish the house.

Sinatra sold the house in 1957 and moved to Tamarisk Country Club. It sat untouched by its new occupant for some twenty years, the redwood facade and built-ins deteriorating through neglect and termites, until it was recently purchased and renovated by landscape architect Marc Sanders. •

"Maybe it's the air, maybe it's the altitude, maybe it's just the place's goddamn karma...."

Above: To repay a favor he owed, Sinatra let the house be used once in a movie, the 1950 Joan Crawford film The Damned Don't Cry, *but restricted filming to exteriors only. The original radio antenna still protrudes from the roof. Overleaf: The master bedroom, at left, looks north to the San Gorgonio Pass. A single motorized door opens the entire living area to the pool.*

William and Marjorie Edris House, 1954

E. Stewart Williams, Architect

Marjorie Edris still lives in the house Stewart Williams designed for her and her late husband, William, in 1954, and it remains one of the architect's favorite projects. The house has been impeccably maintained, every wood surface gleaming and in excellent condition, inside and out. "It's somewhat more sophisticated than Frank Sinatra's house," Williams says, "and an interesting example of how design can be integrated into a site."

The Edrises, who divided the rest of the year between hotel suites in Seattle and New York, had met Williams when they rented neighboring apartments. "We had come out on vacation without a reservation and the town was full," recalls Marjorie Edris. "We found two front rooms in an apartment building where Stewart and his family were living. I don't think the units were even finished, but we moved in anyway and we became good friends." A year later the couple returned to Palm Springs, bought a place, and asked the architect to add a pool. By year three they had found a long lot ("the biggest one my husband could find") and asked him to build their house. "We had the plans in 1953 and we moved in in spring 1954," says Marjorie Edris. "We were very fortunate, we had Stewart all to ourselves — he was the architect and the contractor."

Stewart Williams had first come to the desert on vacation in 1943. His father, Harry, and brother, Roger, had been brought in from Dayton, Ohio, in 1934 to design the village's first commercial venture, the Plaza shopping center. "Julia Carnell, whose husband was the comptroller of National Cash Register, would spend every winter at Nellie Coffman's Desert Inn. Julia knew my father because he was the architect of most of NCR's offices in Dayton, and she asked him and her financial adviser to come out to southern California to search for some real estate — she thought the region would be a good investment," says Stewart Williams. "The Plaza was about the only thing constructed during the Depression. I remember Nellie Coffman saying, 'I don't understand why Julia put the Plaza so far out of town.'"

Williams had spent a year studying in Sweden, where he met his wife, Mari, and he developed a tremendous admiration for Swedish design and the Scandinavian design ethos. "They respect natural materials," he says. "The Swedish Pavilion at the 1939 World's Fair was the only one really full of life."

After being discharged from the army and a spell working for industrial designer Raymond Loewy, Stewart Williams moved to Palm Springs to join the firm Williams and Williams in 1946. "The postwar population was about two thousand. It was a terrible place to establish a practice," he recalls. "And you couldn't earn a cent doing houses. People didn't put that kind of money into Palm Springs then, they were building modest weekend places. I did garages and guest rooms and the occasional house." Apart from his own house, which he built in 1955 and lived in until 1997, Williams designed only about six other private residences. The majority of his commissions, done in conjunction with his

Architecture as an expression of the environment became Stewart Williams's signature. For the Edrises, he excavated some of the site's giant boulders to create the pool and set their vacation house gently onto a level pad above.

"*A building should grow out of a site, not look like a spaceship that has just landed,*" *Williams says. The V-shaped roof, which hovers over the 2,800-square-foot house, was hung from a steel frame.*
Right: The low-lying entrance offers few clues to the panoramic views that are visible from the back of the house.

Top left and right: Williams placed a planter inside the entrance and continued the greenery theme with a divider that separates the dining and living rooms. He designed all the light fixtures, including the iron rods topped with shades inspired by Dixie cups.

Above left and right: The guest room is clad in Douglas fir; the kitchen cabinetry is walnut.

Right: Joists in the living room ceiling were left exposed so that lighting could be installed to spotlight the couple's art collection. "Since it was just a winter home, we didn't hang our best things here," says Marjorie Edris. The Edrises went furniture shopping in Los Angeles, "and we picked everything out in one morning from the same store."

brother or as joint ventures with Clark, Frey, and Chambers, were commercial projects: Coachella Valley Bank (now Great Western) and Santa Fe Savings and Loan (now American Savings), additions to City Hall, the auditorium of Palm Springs High School, the Mountain Station of the Palm Springs Aerial Tramway, Crafton Hills College in Yucaipa, and the Palm Springs Desert Museum.

The Edris House sits on its own promontory overlooking the Coachella Valley. Around it is an alluvial plain of giant boulders that were bulldozed into clusters when the roads were put in. Williams did some excavating to carve out the pool and to create a flat building pad, but he moved as few boulders as possible. "Some of them are twenty feet high. If you moved one, there was another one right behind it. I remember measuring each rock to see how to build."

He tried to set the L-shaped, 2,800-square-foot house gently into its environment. The roof was hung from a steel frame. Except for the west side wall and chimney of native stone, the house was sheathed entirely in wood. He chose first-grade Douglas fir ("well-selected with no knots") that was sandblasted and painted for the ceilings and walls. Folding doors close off the open kitchen. The compact space shimmers with stainless-steel appliances and walnut veneer over plywood. No nails were used.

To light a wall in the living room for the couple's paintings, Williams left a section of the ceiling joists exposed and placed recessed lights flush with the fir beams. The roof floats down into a V from its highest point outside the living room to its lowest point in the dining area and then back up over the kitchen, study, and utility rooms. It hovers independently of the low-set walls, anchored only by the stone chimneypiece. Greenery was introduced in a deep planter on both sides of the entry. A plant-filled divider between the entrance and dining room holds slender iron rods topped with perforated iron shades that Williams designed by punching holes into Dixie cups.

The house is a quiet symphony in browns and green, wood and stone. Outside, where steps between boulders lead down to the pool, only a storage box intrudes against the house's profile; it was made of fir and painted the same color to blend in, and it too is in pristine condition. "That's always been a bone of contention out here," notes Williams. "Some architects think that you can't use wood outside in the desert. That's not true — you just have to use dry wood to start out with and you have to have a dry desert." •

Above and right: The roof hangs independently over the stone wall that defines the guest bedroom at the west end of the house.

Mari and Stewart Williams House, 1956

E. Stewart Williams, Architect

As an expression of the physical and social environment that produced it, architecture has the potential ability of being the greatest art of its time.

— E. Stewart Williams

"I had known John Clark at Cornell and we went to his house for dinner in 1946," recounts Stewart Williams. "After dinner we walked over to this site. There weren't many trees — you could look right across to Desert Hot Springs — and there was a wonderful view of the mountains and stars."

The area was in the northern part of town, where Sally Stevens and Culver Nichols lived in the small caddy house of El Mirador Hotel's former golf course. "After the hotel failed, the Stevens family retained the golf course area, and they didn't want to subdivide the land," Williams says. He became the third architect after John Porter Clark and Albert Frey to be invited to build on 1.3 acres of undeveloped property. "Nichols told me to pace off what I wanted," he says. "I used the line of tamarisks that led to the caddy house as the marker."

A gently sloping lawn is dotted with circles planted with thousands of annuals. Olive trees, dwarf oleander, palo verdes, and African sumac were introduced. The tamarisks shelter the back of the house but offer little protection against the fierce winds that blow through the area. "When the wind blows in spring the tamarisks are useless, so I decided to put up a wall as a windbreak," he says. "The garden wall penetrates the living room — there's a one-foot elevation from the garden — and it curves five feet inward. We poured the whole wall lying down like a sidewalk, then tilted it up. I thought it would be nice to have a roof that floats, so I designed a butterfly roof low on both ends that cantilevers out over three rows of side beams. We eliminated walls where we could to let the landscape flow through and we tried to put one wall of glass in each room. The house is essentially a roof over the garden so the desert can flow through. It was designed to be a shelter in a very hard climate."

Williams was an avowed modernist influenced by the International Style but never a devotee. "It taught you to break loose from traditional forms and invent from the ground up, but it had rigid tenets and rules and regulations. I think architecture should be approached with an open mind." He was drawn to the elegance in Mies van der Rohe's lines. "His houses are more open than Le Corbusier's. Mies had a lovely way of dividing space. He brought in the outdoors, which is a natural thing to do." Williams tried to make all his structures look like they grew out of their site. Earth tones predominate in all his projects, especially in his own house. "I don't like stucco or paint — let the natural beauty of the material be the thing you see on the finish," he says. Floors of polished poured concrete were stained in tobacco brown with a blue-green copper sulphate for a bronze-olive hue, and the steel window frames were stained the same color. The bedroom walls were covered with grass cloth applied on plywood.

Continuing his belief that "environment is an important part of life," Stewart Williams floated a butterfly roof over his own house and brought the garden into the living room. Williams poured the garden wall lying down like a sidewalk, then tilted it into place.

The dining room painting, one of several around the house by the couple's son Geoffrey Williams, reflects "desert washes, tidal flats, and the clear water and coolness of our cabin in Idaho," says Williams.

"We feel very close to nature here. Everything is functional and was designed for a reason." Williams designed the suspended fireplace and most of the furniture, but the original sofa was replaced. "It was too hard," he admits. Behind the living room is a sheltered patio. An evaporative cooler served as the air-conditioning system.

Even exponents of modernism enjoy their creature comforts.

Williams and his wife acted as their own interior designers. He designed some of the furniture, and they added Scandinavian pieces, notably armchairs and side tables by Alvar Aalto. Even exponents of modernism enjoy their creature comforts, however, and he carpeted the bedroom floor and replaced the original couch, which was too hard. Williams and his late wife, Mari, lived in the house from 1956 to 1997. "Architecture is a lousy business," he says. "You've got to have fun — we were making it up as we went along on an architect's salary." •

Above: Tamarisks were supplanted with dwarf oleander, palo verde trees, and African sumac for privacy. Each spring the couple planted thousands of annuals in flower beds. "Far from the traffic and noise of the big city, free from worry and tension, Palm Springs became a Shangri-La, sufficient unto itself, different, unique, full of fun and peace of mind," Stewart Williams wrote.

Left: The dressing area is furnished with classic Alvar Aalto pieces "from one of the first shipments that arrived in the U.S." The walls in the master bedroom were covered in glasscloth and the polished concrete floor was carpeted "because it was too cold," says Williams.

Various Projects, 1947–1971

William F. Cody, Architect

"Bill was Beaux-Arts trained — he had a strong background in classical architecture," relates his brother John Joseph Cody. "Our mother decorated hotels in the Midwest, and on Sunday drives around town she'd test us by asking us to identify the styles of the houses." The Cody family moved from Dayton, Ohio, to Los Angeles in the 1920s. William Francis Cody attended Beverly Hills High and graduated from USC in 1942. A. Quincy Jones, a fellow architect who became dean of architecture at USC, would become a lifelong friend. Cody put himself through college by working for Cliff May, the creator of many of Los Angeles's best ranch-style bungalows, particularly in Brentwood and Pacific Palisades. He enlisted in the navy during the war "and he had a commission, but they kicked him out because of his asthma," says his brother. He opened an office in west Los Angeles near Bundy Drive and Santa Monica Boulevard and worked on a variety of commissions: the Kaiser Aluminum plant, a house in Los Angeles, a mining company office in Morency, Arizona.

Cody moved to Palm Springs in 1944–45 at the invitation of cartoonist and Western artist Jimmy Swinnerton, a fellow asthma sufferer who worked for William Randolph Hearst and had been sent to the Desert Inn for his health. Cody was immediately put to work renovating cottages for Nellie Coffman's hacienda-style hotel. His own first job was the Del Marcos Hotel (1946), which was given a "creditable mention" award in 1949 by the southern California chapter of the American Institute of Architects as an example of new resort hotel architecture. "This building seems to succeed because of its ingenious plan, which appears complicated but is actually orderly and thoughtful. The pleasant residential character of the design is not forced but is consistently a logical expression of the arrangement of space," wrote the judges, who included Eero Saarinen. The "distinguished" award that year was given to the Edgar J. Kaufmann House by Richard Neutra (page 50).

Oilman and entrepreneur Jack Wrather, Walt Disney's partner in the Disneyland Hotel, owned a choice 8½-acre parcel south of town, and Russell Wade, then operating a small real estate business in Palm Springs, suggested that he meet with Cody. At the time Cody was working on his own house, and he used the same steel beams and adobe partitions for the cluster of cottages he came up with for L'Horizon Hotel, the desert getaway for Wrather and his friends. When Thunderbird and Tamarisk country clubs were being developed in the early 1950s, Cody was asked to design the clubhouses and he drew up the original concept for the housing alongside the fairway, the first time that golf courses and houses came into close contact.

Preceding pages: A massive roof overhang juts out from the living room to create an outdoor living space at the 1955 Jorgensen House at Thunderbird Country Club.

Right: For the clubhouse at Eldorado Country Club in Indian Wells, completed in 1959, Cody combined high ceilings, banks of glass windows, carved wood room dividers that separate the lobby and dining room, and spherical glass lights. Arthur Elrod balanced Cody's architecture with low-slung groups of modern furniture.

Cody's own house, built in 1947, was a deft combination of exposed steel beams, adobe walls, and glass. Cody loved the desert. His search for the best combination to combat the heat led to flat roofs, adobe walls, tile floors, and teak. The wall ran around the perimeter in zigzags instead of straight lines. Interior courtyards, reflecting pools, and atriums broke up the spaces. Cody was eliminating the division between indoor and out. To accommodate a growing family, he added two separate guest houses, with one also serving as an office. A canopy of blue glass protected the walkway of black paving stones that ran from the front gate past the carport to the front door. Cody would vary the widths of wood with beams and purlins, paying meticulous attention to each seam and joint. A sunken conversation pit in the middle of the living room, the scene of numerous cocktail parties, had "tiny pinkish-beige tile on the floor and blue tile on the four sides," daughter Lynne Cody says. "Everyone fell in it." An ornate Moroccan lantern hung low over the pit, thick padded cushions covered in dark blue leather surrounded it; interior designer Maurice Martiné came up with a special tray table supported by two long legs that descended into the pit. Outdoors was a giant chessboard based on one at the Racquet Club, two fountains, and an alfresco shower off the master bedroom. Cody collected the art of his friend Jimmy Swinnerton and often worked iron sculptures onto walls or into channels of water in his projects. Above the bed in the master bedroom was a sliding glass panel. "Sleeping there was like camping out at night," Lynne recalls. "One night one of my mother's cats fell on Dad's stomach; the next day he tore out the glass."

A scale model of Cody's own 1947 Palm Springs house. "It was a magical place," says his youngest daughter, Catherine, who is also an architect. "The undulating adobe wall created pockets of gardens. There were three reflecting ponds. Opaque materials were combined with transparent glass. Along with the garden lights illuminating the desert plants, nights were unforgettable."

The wall ran around the perimeter in zigzags instead of straight lines. Interior courtyards, reflecting pools, and atriums broke up the spaces. Cody was eliminating the division between indoor and out.

Cody next turned his attention to country clubs. Thunderbird, Tamarisk, and Eldorado country clubs, the oldest and most exclusive clubs in the desert, were the first golf courses to be sold as residential communities. These gated communities completely changed the way golf courses were designed, and they profoundly altered the way people thought of resort living.

Cody was a master of proportion, and he did some of his most sophisticated work at Eldorado for the clubhouse, guest cottages, and a handful of private houses. He put the already stripped down and slender modern rectangle on a diet and shaved it down to nothingness. Steel allowed him to elongate roof spans. Steel beams became anemic, as slender as his engineers could make them. Joints and door frames seemingly disappeared into the walls ("hush and flush" in Cody parlance). He had water flowing in and out of rooms in channels and reflecting pools below overhangs. He merged living rooms into terraces and gardens. Roofs jutted out twelve feet to shield the walls of glass. Pattern and texture came from tile floors, carved wood panels, and concrete-block screens with geometric motifs, all of which were meticulously designed by Cody to match each other precisely at the seams and angles where the planes met. He was as obsessive about those details — and about architecture in general — as he was unconcerned about his health and appearance. In 1959 Cody was at his peak, designing the Palm Springs Spa, the Palm Springs Library, and Eldorado Country Club at the same time. He would also collaborate with interior designer Arthur Elrod, who had the top design practice in town and the best client list, on a variety of projects in the late 1950s and 1960s.

Robert McCulloch, president of Eldorado, had reluctantly agreed to hire Cody to do the club's guest cottages. "Bob wanted a Beverly Hills architect, but I told him the greatest architect for the desert was Cody," says Russell Wade, former actor, realtor for Eldorado since its inception, and a great friend of Cody. Eldorado was completed in 1959, in time to host its first Ryder Cup match. It became associated with old money, with Dwight and Mamie Eisenhower, and a gentle golf course "that allows you to play into your nineties," avers Wade.

Portuguese cork trees and palms follow rows of fountains that lead to the loggia and carved walnut front doors. Glass block on one side of the facade lets light into the men's locker room. In the lobby of the 60,000-square-foot clubhouse, tall room dividers of wood and concrete with recurring geometric motifs break up the space and provide the textural background; high ceilings merge with large banks of glass windows. Amid the lobby's groupings of low, modern furniture devised by interior designer Arthur Elrod — two-seater couch, coffee table, and facing armchairs — were a carved wood console and a gilt mirror from William Randolph Hearst's estate. The dining room overlooks four fairway directions — the fourth, ninth, thirteenth, and eighteenth holes. Cody let the Santa Rosa Mountains provide the dramatic backdrop. The dining room's lights were clusters of fancifully

The hallway of the Cannon House looked out to the terrace, pool, and golf course of the Eldorado Country Club. Cody conjured a symmetrical symphony of perfectly matched Spanish quarry tile for the floors and a ceiling of lacquered redwood siding.

designed glass globes and spheres hanging at different lengths; the bar was all teak. A private ban-quet room with a mosaic wall is dedicated to the club's much admired, longtime resident, Dwight Eisenhower. At Eldorado, Cody would refine the concept of an exclusive country club and rectify mis-takes he'd made at Thunderbird. One of the most logical additions at Eldorado was a lower level excavated underneath the clubhouse restaurant for dropping off and storing golf carts. "At Thunder-bird the cart stop was a ways away, so people had to wait," explains Wade. "This way, the starter calls and the cart comes right up."

It was for his private clients, though, that Cody pulled out all the stops, conjuring sophisticated statements of his architectural philosophy, "which was always intuitive and spontaneous," says his friend George Hasslein, the founding dean of architecture at California Polytechnic at San Luis Obispo, where Cody's archives are housed. "He was an emotional architect, not a rational one. His life wasn't very rational either. He was strongest in the feeling for a structure — not the structure itself. His challenge to engineers was how thin could he make the roof slabs and beams and still have the house stand up." The Robert Cannon House (1959) and the J. B. Shamel House (1961) at Eldorado are considered Cody's best work and won him awards from the American Institute of Architects and the American Institute of Steel Construction.

The Cannon House, which won a 1963 award from the southern California chapter of the AIA, was protected from the sun by a twelve-foot-deep overhang that ran the length of the kitchen and living room. Furnishings were designed by Maurice Martiné.

"He was strongest in the feeling for a structure—not the the structure itself."

For the J. B. Shamel House at Eldorado, considered Cody's best work and since razed, Cody continued to obliterate the difference between indoors and out. He pushed new technology to its limits to get the steel roof span, frame, and columns as thin as possible. A convex wall in the living room contained a slender fireplace. The kitchen had views of the Santa Rosa Mountains.

JULIUS SHULMAN

"His challenge to engineers was how thin could he make the roof slabs and beams and still have the house stand up."

JULIUS SHULMAN

Steel magnate Earle M. Jorgensen and his wife, Marion, live in a low-slung ranch house in Bel-Air that had been decorated by Billy Haines, with his Chippendale and oriental blend of folding screens, low chairs, and long, narrow tables, where four election-night parties for the Reagans were celebrated. For the Jorgensens' Palm Springs getaway at the Thunderbird Country Club, completed in April 1955, Cody designed a horizontal house with an opposition roof that exuded a powerful individuality through its simple but meticulous detailing.

Marion Jorgensen had hired Cody after seeing a house he had completed nearby, but she says he had "the craziest ideas," and that she rejected his suggestion of "front doors with hinges down the middle." Cody would use conventional materials, but he delighted in pushing technology. The huge overhang projection outside the living room, supported by four solid posts, dropped all pretense of being a mere extension of the interior. The outdoor terrace graduated and became a room in its own right. The four-bedroom house encompassed 3,300 square feet; the exterior took up 2,500 square feet. With its proximity to the pool and a radiant view of the golf course and mountains, the terrace was the most visible and heavily trafficked area in the house. Helen Conway, who had worked for Billy Haines before setting up her own design business on Sunset Boulevard, had all the furniture custom made. The upholstery and curtains were woven from Peruvian fabrics, some with a thunderbird motif worked in. The Jorgensens used the house one season and sold it lock, stock, and barrel in 1956 to the Mavis family, the current owners, who have kept it the way it was.

Steel beams became anemic, as slender as his engineers could make them. Joints and door frames seemingly disappeared into the walls ("hush and flush" in Cody parlance).

The swimming pool of the Jorgensen House, which had shallow steps that ran all the way across its bottom, is reflected in the deep terrace overhang.

Cool terrazzo floors run from the hallway to the living room. The Jorgensens worked with designer Helen Conway, who created all the furnishings, including using an oversize boxspring mattress for the Hawaiian-style sofa. Their neighbor on one side was Lucille Ball, on the other the chairman of Ford. The Jorgensens sold the furnished house after one season to the Mavis family.

Interior designer Harold Broderick had long admired a house Cody built in the Movie Colony in 1962. Broderick calls it the "pavilion house" since it consists of a series of individual living pavilions united under a twenty-four-foot shake roof. Broderick and his former partner, Arthur Elrod, arrived in town in 1954 after working together at W & J Sloane in San Francisco and opened an instantly successful interior design studio in the desert. Their showroom on Palm Canyon Drive carried the top fabric and furniture lines of the day—they were the exclusive representatives for Baker and Widdicomb furnishings and hence T. H. Robsjohn-Gibbings' line of Greek Revival furniture. "We used Widdicomb furniture at the Lucy and Desi Arnaz House at Thunderbird that Paul Williams designed," Broderick says. Many of their clients asked them to work on primary residences in Beverly Hills and Oklahoma as well as their vacation homes.

The designers first met Bill Cody when he was building in Las Palmas and they were sharing the same contractor. Cody had completed a house for Ralph Abernathy and his second wife, Madge Phillips, and would continue to collaborate with Elrod until the early 1970s. "Mrs. Abernathy was still living here when I saw it," says Broderick. "You couldn't see out. The property was completely over-planted and there were three tiers of window drapes on brass poles — blackout liners, brocades, silk drapes. The floors were covered in oriental rugs. Madge was a portrait painter, and all the walls were covered with her paintings."

Over the past eight years Broderick has simplified the house and let Cody's sure touches come through. "We just cleaned it up — the trim was bright white, we brought it back to neutral —and repolished the terrazzo floors. It was a forerunner of a contemporary house in the desert," he adds. "Cody used walls of glass and immaculate detailing — the wood paneling on the walls matches the wood on the ceiling."

"His proportions were wonderful," says current owner and interior
designer Hal Broderick, who opened a design studio in Palm Springs
in the mid-1950s with Arthur Elrod.
*Overleaf: For the Abernathys, Cody devised a series of airy high-
ceilinged pavilions around a pool.* COURTESY PALM SPRINGS LIFE.

Above: Mitered glass follows the contours of the kitchen's brick wall.

Left: "The living room is thirty feet square with a twenty-six-foot ceiling," Broderick says. "We bought the house from Madge Phillips Abernathy and just had to clean it up a bit to let Cody's wood details come to the forefront."

Right: "Cody loved being outdoors and he wanted nothing to interfere with the views," says Broderick. A sculpture stands in the atrium.

Cody's offices (he had others in San Francisco and Phoenix) would be asked to plan golf resorts in California, Arizona, Mexico, Havana, and Monte Carlo. He worked with associates on a multitude of projects, and his desert office was a training ground for a new generation of architects — Donald Wexler, Ric Harrison, and Frank Urrutia, among them — but he never formed any partnerships. "He was too strong a personality," says his brother. Cody enhanced his reputation with his habit of working on job sites during the day, heading out for a cocktail or two after work, and heading back to the office to work late into the night. He loved practical jokes and had "a huge belly laugh that sounded like Santa Claus," says Russell Wade. "He looked like Jackie Gleason and was as silly as Robin Williams," adds his daughter Lynne. But Cody was passionate about architecture and he served on the Palm Springs Planning Commission from 1960 to 1965, determined to support construction that benefited the desert. As president of its planning collaborative from 1965 to 1967 he tried his utmost to protect the environment and the area from what he considered architectural mediocrity.

Many of Cody's buildings have been remodeled beyond recognition or razed. He had pushed structures to their limits and allowed little room for future additions. The roof of his own house was only four inches thick. Engineers and contractors were usually unable to modify or expand on his designs. The elegant Palm Springs Spa Hotel (1959), on the site of the Agua Caliente hot springs and mud baths, went from aqua to pink and is now a spa casino. The Springs Restaurant, one of his favorite projects, where informal meetings of the Palm Springs chapter of the AIA were conducted, was torn down and is now an empty lot. The Shamel House at Eldorado was torn down in 1993. But the Palm Springs Library Center and St. Theresa's Church, where the funeral services for former mayor Sonny Bono were held, are still in excellent condition. His last projects were a house at Eldorado and the Palm Springs Tennis Club's hotel and condos.

In 1971 Bill Cody suffered a debilitating stroke; he died six years later at the age of sixty-two. Architect Hugh Kaptur, who designed several houses in Palm Springs, commented, "He was an architect's architect. He had a special way of using natural materials and combining different materials like glass, which disappears into the ceiling and floor as though it wasn't there. He pioneered what has become known as desert architecture. He was one of the greats who will be in the history books." Adds his brother John Cody, "He was a natural talent who understood proportion better than anyone." •

"He was an emotional architect, not a rational one. His life wasn't very rational either."

The original design by Cody in association with Wexler and
Harrison for the Palm Springs Spa, which is owned by the Agua
Caliente Indians, featured a water channel of aqua tile leading to
the entrance. "Bill Cody was a spirited, generous man as well as
innovative in his architecture," wrote his friend, architect A. Quincy
Jones. "All of this comes through in the character of his work."

J. J. Robinson House, 1957

A. Quincy Jones and Frederick E. Emmons, Architects

Jerome Robinson, owner of a parking meter company in Chicago, and his wife hired A. Quincy Jones to design their winter retreat after seeing his house for their friend Louis Golan. To fully utilize the corner lot on an acre, Jones placed the L-shaped house close to the road but angled it toward the landscaped garden and the mountains.

A low wall of opaque glass shields the bedroom wing from the street. Jones paid careful attention to the transition from bright sun to cool interior and he created a ceremonial procession from the motor court: A concrete porte cochere leads to two black doors that open onto a small low-ceilinged entry defined by a pierced fretwork walnut screen. His sensitivity to color meant that paint was mixed and remixed until all surfaces appeared identical in color as the sun passed overhead. Fossilized rocks were applied unevenly to several walls. A cove-lit clerestory runs parallel to the long living room's stone wall, sinking soft light into dark corners.

The living room was broken up by the honey-colored stone walls, a rectangular fireplace that jutted outdoors as a stone wall, and a low ceiling that defined the dining area. One of the most distinctive features was a fully equipped step-down wet bar conceived by Jones initially for the Henry Hathaway and Golan houses in Beverly Hills. Jones reasoned that during parties the host needed something to do, so he provided an area that contained an oven, barbeque, sink, and fridge. The lower floor allowed the host to stand at eye level with his guests, who were seated behind the Formica-topped counter. The far end of the living room ends in an outdoor terrace shaded by trellis-work. Concentric stone circles were placed on the lawn around the pool for outdoor entertaining.

The J. J. Robinson House, set on just over an acre, faces west toward the mountains. Quincy Jones, who always sought to maximize a home's comfort level, designed a concrete inverted U-shaped roof overhang that protects the long hallway and master bedroom from the afternoon sun.

The house was placed close to the street to take full advantage of the site.
A wall of opaque glass shields the master bedroom wing and leads to the
porte cochere and front door, which are kept in shadow.

Top: A cove-lit clerestory illuminates the dark corners of the dining room and the sunken wet bar, a concept Jones had developed to allow the host to be able to mix drinks and tend to an indoor barbecue while talking with guests.

Above: Jones, who sought an efficient circulation, used a low horizontal ceiling and a strong vertical fireplace that extends outdoors to separate the long living room and draw the eye to the outdoor terrace.

Right: An open terrace at the far end of the living room still has the furniture that was installed in 1957 by interior designer Helen Franklin, as well as an early-nineteenth-century Portuguese azulejos tile set against the trellis.

His sensitivity to color meant that paint was mixed and remixed until all surfaces appeared identical in color as the sun passed overhead.

Jones developed a concrete U-shaped roof overhang suited for the climate that he used for the rear elevation of the Robinson House, mainly to protect the master bedroom from the afternoon sun. When he collaborated in 1958 with decorator Billy Haines on Romanoff's, the popular Palm Springs restaurant, he would repeat the same overhang. The materials in the living areas were restrained — steel frame, plaster, stone, river pebbles, terrazzo floors. For the bedroom wing, Jones varied the surfaces. Distressed wood was used for the hallway closets. The narrow hallway has a herringbone-patterned tile floor, shutters with thin vertical slats on one side, and a combed plaster wall on the other. Metallic wallpaper was hung in the daughter's bedroom. Olivewood veneer was used in the office/sitting room.

Helen Franklin, who had done the interiors of the Hathaway and Golan houses, was hired by the art-collecting Robinsons to decorate the house.

In 1975 Robinson sold his company and retired to the desert. The master bedroom and bathrooms were expanded, an office added, and the interiors redone. Nine years ago private art dealers Gordon Locksley and Dr. George Shea bought the house and its furnishings from Mrs. Robinson. •

Left: The hallway that connects the entry to the master wing is paved with herringbone-patterned tile and has shutters made of thin vertical slats. On the combed plaster wall is a 1987 Dan Flavin fluorescent light sculpture. Right: A walnut fretwork screen separates the entry from the living room.

Frey House II, 1963

Albert Frey, Architect

After living on the valley floor for twenty-five years and staring at the mountains, Albert Frey decided to seek a vantage point in the hills so that he could gaze over the valley. "I thought for a change I'd like to look down," he says.

Frey had fled Zurich and its stifling Beaux-Arts architectural environment in the early 1920s for the sophisticated modernism of Paris, where he studied with Le Corbusier for nine months. ("Swiss architects were repeating designs that had been there for years, and that didn't interest me," he said. "I was at the point of becoming an engineer instead of an architect.") His interest in improving every-day living through affordable design led him to the United States, "where factories and industrial constructions, even grain silos, showed very advanced techniques, such as steel." He made his way to New York in 1930, where he met A. Lawrence Kocher, the managing editor of *Architectural Record*, who would become Frey's first partner. Together they created the now renowned Aluminaire House, an experimental light steel and aluminum prototype of an attractive low-cost prefabricated house, which was built full-scale for the 1931 Allied Arts and Building Products Exhibition. Kocher's brother was the first doctor and pharmacist in Palm Springs, and an invitation from Dr. J. J. Kocher to design the Kocher-Samson office building drew Frey to the desert in 1934. After a brief return to New York to work as a contributing designer with the architects of the Museum of Modern Art, Frey settled in Palm Springs permanently in 1939.

Frey built his first house for himself in 1941 on a lot next to John Porter Clark, his second partner. The house started as a sixteen-by-twenty, 320-square-foot, wood-frame rectangle that cost $1,800 to build and became his laboratory for experimenting with products — corrugated metals, aluminum, steel, and asbestos boards — that were then becoming standardized and readily available. Palm Springs was the ideal locale for someone fascinated with putting into practice the materials and ideas that could contribute to a simpler way of living. Frey sheathed the house in corrugated metal, used walls of glass to make the volume seem larger, and, influenced by Mies van der Rohe, experimented with defining outdoor spaces as extensions of indoor rooms. A long, low, horizontal glass wall expanded out from the living room toward the pool. He put in a circular fireplace of metal "so that everyone can enjoy it" and a hanging dining table suspended from the ceiling with cables crossed at right angles to prevent it from twisting. A round second-story bedroom added later had telescope-like windows covered in sheet metal that made the place look like a B-movie spaceship. He had calculated the amount of light each opening received and carefully sited each window for views and air circulation.

By the time he built his second house in Palm Springs, Albert Frey was adept at fitting a structure into its natural terrain. The 1964 house at the top of a private road perches amid the natural outcroppings of the mountainous terrain.

Frey's second house was simpler but more advanced in its use of materials. He spent five years searching for a site "from one end of town to another," finally settling on a steep arid lot two hundred feet up Tahquitz Canyon. "I don't think the owner could figure out how to build on it," the ninety-four-year-old architect says. He first constructed a retaining wall to create a deck; under it is a carport that houses his Reliant K-car with the license plate ALUMI; the carport supports the swimming pool above. "This was a different project entirely than house number one," Frey says. "I wasn't in any hurry and I did a careful survey of the grounds; I put strings up to see where the house would go."

Central to the site is a massive gray granite boulder that Frey incorporated into the house; it serves as an effective room divider between the living/dining area and his bedroom. "I live alone and it's not worth making a fire, so instead of a fireplace the rock is the focal point." He anchored I-beams with fiberglass insulation to the rock, installed an aluminum channel to position the glass, and then used colored mortar to fill in the gap.

The roof, overhang, ceiling, and walls are all of low-cost, low-maintenance aluminum with baked-enamel finishes of bronze, sage green, and blue to match the surroundings (the finishes were baked on in the factory and never have to be retouched). "The weather is too hot for wood. Metal doesn't retain heat — it cools off in minutes," says Frey, who championed aluminum and steel. "The typical wood-frame and stucco house stays hot and keeps cracking." Yellow drapes, lined inside with reflective Mylar, were inspired by the encelia that blooms in yellow clusters in the hills. The gray cement floor matches the rocks — the house is supposed to blend seamlessly into nature.

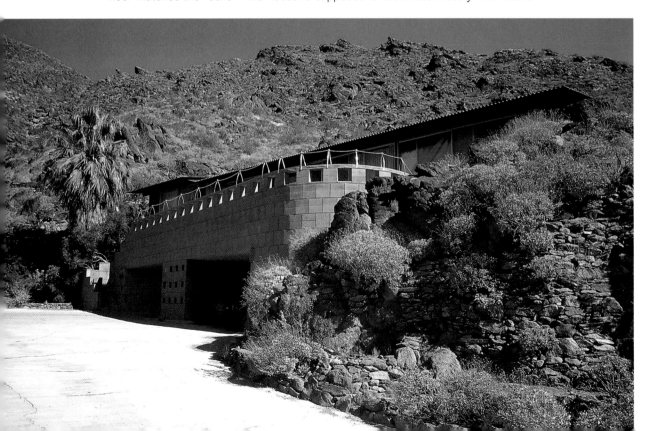

Above: A metal overhang— "unlike wood, metal doesn't retain heat in the desert," Frey says—was essential to protect the glass windows. The house, which sits 220 feet above the city, was the valley's highest residence when it was built.

Left: Frey first constructed the concrete retaining wall to house the carport and support a pool above.

Above: Aluminum panels with factory baked-on finishes and curtains the color of the encilia that blooms outside combine to make the house blend into its surroundings.

Left: "The house is anchored to the rock," says Frey, who used the massive grey granite boulder as a divider between the living room and sleeping area. "The only way to think ideas through is to write a book," says Frey, who published In Search of a Living Architecture *in 1959.*

137

"They called it a crazy house and said, 'We guess you know what you're doing.'"

"During World War II planes couldn't take off from Los Angeles because of fog in the morning, so they built a landing strip here for the air force," Frey explains. "They would arrive in the late afternoon and take off early the next morning. A lot of aluminum was produced for the planes, so there was plenty around after the war." All the aluminum companies like Alcoa were making corrugated metals. Frey found the four-by-eight-foot panels of Philippine mahogany for the cabinetry in a lumberyard. "I took some Cabot's Stain Wax and added some white pigment for a driftwood effect," he says, "and brushed it over the wood once." The kitchen countertop is one seamless piece of stainless steel with a round opening for trash. Every element used in the house's composition was meant to be long-lasting. With partner John Porter Clark, and later Robson Chambers, Frey would contribute a unique modernist vision to the buildings of Palm Springs. His hyperbolic paraboloid roof of the Tramway Gas Station (1964) announced the entrance to the city. The history of Palm Springs architecture is rooted in collaboration, since the firms were too small to take on larger-scale projects alone. Clark, Frey, and Chambers — in association with Stewart Williams and Roger Williams — would work together on the major public works projects of the city in its formative stages. They created the look for City Hall, virtually all the schools in the Coachella Valley, the Palm Springs High School, and the Palm Springs Aerial Tramway.

Reaction at City Hall to Frey's own house was mixed. "They called it a crazy house and said, 'We guess you know what you're doing,'" he recalls. "So they gave me a permit. But I would have a very hard time building this today." •

Above left: Built-in concrete benches by the front door are for sunbathing. Shallow steps lead into the pool. Above right: A detail of the concrete block at the foot of the stairs. Right: Frey applied a stain wax to the Philippine mahogany walls and chose sage green and blue finishes for the corrugated aluminum ceiling.

Steel Developmental Houses, 1962

Wexler and Harrison, Architects

Original interiors: Harold Broderick of Arthur Elrod Associates. Original landscaping: David Hamilton

By the 1960s, steel was becoming the material of choice for architects in the desert. "There's nothing that can destroy it," says Donald Wexler, who with his partner, Ric Harrison, designed a model house for a proposed subdivision of steel housing. "Steel doesn't warp or shrink, it's light and resistant to earthquakes." Steel was also low maintenance, termite-proof, and the galvanized roof never had to be replaced. But steel wasn't as cheap as wood, and steel interiors didn't always look as appealingly warm as wood.

A large sandy tract behind the Riviera Hotel and the Palm Springs Racquet Club — a pleasant area of many cul-de-sacs developed by George Alexander and his son, Robert — became the testing site for steel developmental houses. The Alexanders were among the largest developers and contractors in the desert in the 1960s before they and their wives were killed in a small airplane crash. Their signature home style was a suburban A-frame bungalow that was given an urbane eighteen-foot-high butterfly ceiling, clerestories that allow in plenty of light, gently sloping roofs, shaded parking spaces, and plenty of overhangs and ornamental screens to fend off the heat.

The majority of the Alexanders' houses were designed by Los Angeles architects Palmer and Krisel. The exception was a row of seven experimental steel houses developed by U.S. Steel in conjunction with Calcor Corporation of Huntington Park, California, and architects Donald A. Wexler and Ric Harrison.

U.S. Steel was supporting many diverse housing projects, obviously interested in researching and developing new outlets for its product, and study houses were an excellent venue to attract consumers' interest and judge their reaction to new products. The study houses, which typically were published in *Architectural Record*, *Arts and Architecture*, the *Los Angeles Times Home* magazine, and international trade journals, weren't commercial projects, but they could become commercial if the ideas proved popular. The houses provided an excellent opportunity to demonstrate how, in contrast to traditional materials, new materials — aluminum, steel, plastic — were cheaper, safer, and longer lasting. After the seven steel houses had been built in Palm Springs, one was erected in Palm Beach Gardens, Florida.

A carport is next to the entrance of an all-steel house designed in 1962 by Wexler and Harrison for the Alexander Construction Company. Developed by U.S. Steel and Calcor Corporation, the model houses elevated steel to new heights. The prefabricated homes could be assembled on-site in three days, were energy-efficient, and were resistant to earthquakes and termites.

Wexler was in Los Angeles on vacation after graduating from the University of Minnesota in 1950 when he called Richard Neutra's office on a whim to apply for a job. He didn't think he had a hope of seeing his hero, but Neutra interviewed him and offered him a position. "Neutra was at his height then — designing Los Angeles County's Hall of Records, his biggest public project. I worked on Elysian Park Heights — a public-housing scheme in Chavez Ravine that never happened and is now Dodger Stadium," says Wexler, who worked at Neutra's office for eight to nine months. When Wexler heard about a job at Tamarisk Country Club in 1952, he called its architect, Bill Cody, went out to Palm Springs to meet him, and was hired.

Wexler and Harrison met while working at Cody's office. Wexler already had experience working with steel, which he saw as a natural complement to the concrete and glass he was already using in his commissions, which ranged from the Palm Springs Airport (1965) to the Desert Water Agency (1978). "The school district thought their buildings were too expensive, so they asked me to see what I could do," recalls Wexler. "I met Bernie Perlin, who was the vice president and chief engineer for Calcor, and we started working together. We developed schools sponsored by U.S. Steel and then I did some experimenting with these model houses. We weren't doing modernism — just following the 'desert design' that all the architects here in the 1950s were doing."

The 1,400-square-foot prefabricated steel house came with a price tag of $13,000 to $17,000, depending on interior finishes and landscaping, and took three days to assemble on site. The lot was extra. Three basic roof styles were offered; the only ornamentation was a folded plate roof that zigzagged over the living room.

A typical layout for the steel house had a living room, a dining room, two bedrooms, and two bathrooms. The core of the house contained the kitchen and bathrooms; around the core, the size of the other rooms was totally flexible. The house could be expanded as needed; nonbearing walls made it easy to reconfigure living areas. "The center is all one piece," says Wexler. "The walls come in big sections and are bolted into a concrete slab foundation. All the standing walls could be customized. And the interior finish was drywall to make people feel more comfortable."

Right: Wexler had worked with Neutra in Los Angeles, and in a nod to his hero he added a spider-leg post in the backyard patio area.
Far Right: A pane of glass between the exterior wall and the room divider lets light filter gently into the master bedroom. The room divider also functions as the bedroom closet.

The house could be expanded as needed; nonbearing walls made it easy to reconfigure living areas.

*Left: Owner Jim Moore discovered the original terrazzo
floors under shag carpet and furnished the living room
with such period pieces as a Knoll coffee table.*
*Above: The central core of the 1,400-square-foot house,
which included the kitchen and bathrooms, came in one
section, but the layout of the living and sleeping areas
was totally flexible.*

The architects used an inverted U-shaped roof and wide over-hang for the living area that overlooks the pool. "The only materials I ever used were steel, concrete, and glass," says Wexler, "and they are all appropriate to the desert climate."

Wexler used the same design principles that he had applied to his own post-and-beam house: He made the model as open as possible, and merged indoor and outdoor living — each bedroom has its own small walled patio. Off the dining area is a rear patio that contains a built-in barbeque area and offers a private garden corner. In a nod to Neutra, an exposed beam juts out in spider-leg fashion. Wexler inserted opaque glass panels next to the living room partition (which doubles on the reverse side as the closet in the bedroom hallway) so that the partition didn't directly abut the wall and light could filter in. He had thought of including a freestanding metal fireplace. But, as he explains, "a fireplace is based on the infiltration of air, and since steel has zero tolerance, we were afraid that the house wouldn't have any air infiltration. How do you tell people to open a window every time they light a fire? It was a problem, so we decided to eliminate the fireplace."

If middle-class families went along with the concept of a factory-built house that had a flexible floor plan, the Alexanders were prepared to develop ninety lots of steel housing. But during the design process the manufacturer raised the price of steel. "The Alexanders wouldn't have any of it — they refused to pay more," says Wexler. "And someone had to be the pioneer. They were very powerful, and all the other developers were watching them to see what would happen. Steel got priced out, so the movement never caught on."

The seven experimental houses that were built are gradually being renovated. The model house, which had interiors by Hal Broderick of Arthur Elrod Associates, has been returned to a simple sophistication by New York–based magazine editor Jim Moore. •

Above: A scale model shows how the nonbearing walls around the core could be easily moved to change the layout of living and sleeping areas. Bedrooms were fourteen feet square and the living room twenty-two by fourteen feet. The seven steel houses built in Palm Springs were all designed by Wexler and Harrison.
Left: A folded steel plate was one of three roof types offered.

"We weren't doing modernism — just following the 'desert design' that all the architects here in the 1950s were doing."

Samuel and Luella Maslon House, 1963
Richard Neutra, Architect

A passion for golf and contemporary art came together in a house Richard Neutra started in 1960 for Minneapolis lawyer Samuel Maslon and his wife, Luella, at Tamarisk Country Club.

The couple spent a lot of time in Los Angeles — they had a house there and were familiar with Neutra's work. "Palm Springs was a great area, and when we decided to build we called him. He was a temperamental, conceited man but very likable and his wife was charming," recalls Luella Maslon, who spends eight months of the year in the desert. "But we weren't interested in a 'Neutra' house — we wanted something that combined our ideas with his and elements of Frank Lloyd Wright."

The couple had some specific requests: They wanted immediate access to the pool, an indoor barbeque, and as much natural and recessed light as possible for their paintings. Neutra rebuffed other suggestions. "He wasn't keen on a fireplace in the bedroom, and he was right," says Maslon. "It's not all it's cracked up to be — too much smoke and soot."

Everything was designed to emphasize the physical setting of fairway greenery and the couple's substantial and growing art collection — African masks alongside Giacometti sculptures and contemporary paintings, all amassed by Luella Maslon based "on what I liked and could afford. It didn't matter about the period."

Neutra extended the roofline to protect the couple's art collection and used the same roof motif for the front entrance (right) as well as in the rear (left), where the iron beam terminates in his signature spider-leg support.

Preceding pages: Kenneth Armitage's Three Standing Figures *is near the deep corner pocket that becomes a natural outdoor extension of the living and family rooms at the Maslon House at Tamarisk Country Club. "Everything was designed for the art— nothing was static," says Luella Maslon.*

Top: Frank Stella's Damascus Gate, *1969, hangs in the long
entrance hall. In the living room is Andy Warhol's 1972 silkscreen
of Luella Maslon, Giacometti's* Femme de Venise, *1956, and a 1986
John Chamberlain chrome sculpture, foreground.*
*Above: Neutra designed all the built-in cabinetry and the barbecue
for the dining room. Behind the table is Jasper Johns's* The Four
Seasons, *1989. In the den, foreground, stands Robert Rauschenberg's*
Wheel *plate.*
*Right: Neutra varied the lighting in the lowered ceiling and soffits
in the guest room hallway.*

There were about ten houses on Tamarisk's fairway when the Maslons dropped their modernist design onto two acres with a desirable mountain view. "It was the first substantial house here and it made a sophisticated statement," she says. "The fact that we'd build a house of this quality made the other residents more relaxed and confident about their design ideas."

Neutra, who had worked with Frank Lloyd Wright in the 1920s, responded with a flat-roofed house that is opened to the garden and fairway with spider-leg supports that extended the roof over the patio. The U-shaped plan placed the kitchen and services to the left next to the garage, the living areas and master bedroom/office facing the golf course, and the guest rooms in a self-contained wing to the right. A long entrance hall acts as a gallery for large-scale artworks and leads between the living and dining rooms and the master bedroom and office. Outside the living room and den the overhang creates a deep corner pocket that functions as an outdoor living area. The low-lying house worked equally well for the couple whether they were alone or had visiting children and grand-children.

Neutra created welcome details for the vacation house. The den/dining room has a built-in hi-fi system, an indoor barbeque with shelves for steaks and charcoal, partitions that open to the scullery, folding doors that conceal a steam table, and a wet bar. He ended bookcases short of their maximum height and filled the space with mirrors to create the illusion of an uninterrupted floating canopy. A terrazzo floor helped give a cooling effect. It was a smartly designed house intended for a family. "It's very practical and easy to take care of," says Luella Maslon. "Neutra knew we were novices at build-ing and he made us add extra rooms to prepare for when our children grew and demanded different amenities. Everything he predicted came true." •

Outside is a large chrome sculpture by Yacov Agam; on the card table is the maquette. Jean Arp's Shell for a Deity, *1954, stands by the ten-foot high windows. The exterior room pocket, sheltered by a deep overhang, has oriental rugs that make it function as an extension of the living room.*

"He was a temperamental, conceited man but very likable and his wife was charming."

Max Palevsky House, 1970

Craig Ellwood, Architect

Craig Ellwood and Max Palevsky met in 1965 when Ellwood designed the award-winning plant/administration/engineering complex for Scientific Data Systems in El Segundo, California. "It was done in an international, hard-edged, modern, Mies style, which was a style I grew up with in Chicago — it seems right," says Palevsky, who founded SDS in 1961, which was acquired by Xerox in 1969. Palevsky retired as director and chairman of the executive committee of Xerox in 1972 and became a supporter and active collector of contemporary art.

In 1970 he commissioned the structural engineer and designer to build a vacation house on what local architect Stewart Williams calls "the best site in Palm Springs." The site abuts the mountainside, with sweeping views east and south of the Coachella Valley in an alluvial area dominated by massive boulders. "Behind us is a runoff ravine and at the top is a waterfall," Palevsky says. "When it rains, the water sweeps down and land is washed away. George Alexander got the city and state to build a dam and then he bought up the land below it and developed the area using five basic house designs. A lot of movie people moved there — Donna Reed, Dinah Shore, Kirk Douglas. My wife and I looked at a number of lots and we had to make a critical choice: Build on a flat lot down below where it stays light longer or get a lot on the hillside where the sun sets behind the mountain earlier. We decided on the hillside because it's more private."

In the entrance of the Palevsky House, Barbara Hepworth's Square Forms, *1963–64, stands at the top of the pathway that passes between the outside wall and the guest rooms at left.*

Palevsky knew from the start that he wanted a classical piece of architecture, and he and Ellwood traveled to Morocco in search of inspiration. "One of the sights that impressed us were walled houses where everything could be put into a central courtyard and locked up at night. Walls were constructed of big boulders and rubble," Palevsky recalls. "We thought we'd try to get that effect, but it would have been too expensive and the plan didn't really fit Ellwood's more classical aesthetic. So we kept the notion of the wall and made the side with the view all glass."

Ellwood had been designing steel-framed structures in Los Angeles since 1949 and by the early 1960s had absorbed the lessons of symmetry and volume in Mies van der Rohe's work. The long white pavilion hunches low on its site, an unobtrusive presence against the rocky hillside. Behind the glass entrance screen, a path leads around the central square block that consists of four identical guest bedrooms, two on each side. A wall of white-painted brick, punctuated by openings with vertical slats, runs the entire length of the house to the east, defining its outer, most exposed side and providing a protective envelope. To the west is the mountain. The south end of the property ends at a ledge, where the wall of brick wraps around to meet a wall of glass. The main house, which sits on an east-west axis perpendicular to the entrance, is a simple construction: Side walls support steel beams, and glass panels are hung from the beams. "The universal reaction was that it's crazy to use steel in the desert, why not use wood, it's much cheaper," says Palevsky. "But steel is easy to maintain. And you can't get that clear roof span with wood."

Craig Ellwood used the hillside's massive boulder clusters to
stabilize the house, and then created a level ledge for the classical
pavilion that hunches unobtrusively against the mountain.

...a vacation house on what local architect Stewart Williams calls "the best site in Palm Springs."

As in classical villas, a central rectangular courtyard sits in the center of the property, providing an interlude between the guest house and main house. Strategically planted ficus in pots and bougainvillea line one side of the courtyard. None of the plants around the house were introduced at random — they are placed to ensure total privacy. Standing quietly in the courtyard's heart, instead of a fountain, is a first-century Roman column of concrete with a marble veneer. "I own some antiquities, and I saw the column lying on the floor in a London gallery," Palevsky recounts. "J. Paul Getty had bought it but he hadn't paid for it. The column makes the inner court — it provides scale."

Ellwood bulldozed some of the boulders on the naturally sloping lot and used fill from the inner courtyard to the edge of the property to level the site. The remaining boulders stabilized the house. Massive floor-to-ceiling sliding glass doors open the living areas onto the interior courtyard and the outdoor terrace.

Much of the furniture was built in, especially in the walnut-paneled master bedroom where Ellwood devised a headboard complete with an intercom system and electronic controls for the drapes and lights. The house and guest rooms are furnished with iconic examples of mid-century modern design — Breuer chairs, Eames lounge chairs and ottomans, George Nelson benches, Saarinen tables, Richard Schultz outdoor furniture around the pool. "This is the third incarnation of the interiors," Palevsky says. "I started out using Mexican furniture — Craig almost had a heart attack. But I was into Spanish revival, and I thought I could put a touch of it into the house. I don't remember what the second look was, but I have no intention of touching anything again."

Palevsky's collection of contemporary art includes works by Roy Lichtenstein, Donald Judd, Andy Warhol, Ettore Sottsass, and Alexander Calder. "It's taken twenty-seven years for everything to settle," he says. "It's hard to do a house and get it right so nothing is bothersome. It's a particularly good house for children because nothing is breakable. I have six kids who grew up here, and we had a lot of fun." •

Above: The pathway leads into the central courtyard, where a first- to second-century-A.D. Roman marble column holds court.
Left: To the right of the living area's geometric mantel is Donald Judd's 1980 ten-unit wall sculpture with panels of red anodized aluminum. A glass work by Ettore Sottsass is on the Roy McMakin coffee table.
Right: Roy Lichtenstein's 1992 Wallpaper with Blue Floor Interior *hangs in the dining area.*

Above: Ellwood devised a headboard with built-in electronic controls for the lights and drapes in the master bedroom. Nearby are an Eames recliner and a George Nelson bench. Top right: The sunken tiled tub adjoining the bedroom looks out the south-facing wall of glass to views of the valley. Bottom right: A 1967 series of Warhol's silkscreened Marilyns lines the bedroom's walnut-paneled wall.

The exterior wall, punctuated by openings with vertical slats, wraps around the pool and spa, where the red, yellow, and blue of Alexander Calder's The Blackboard, 1970, are echoed in the classic Richard Schultz outdoor furniture. "I was very active in the antiwar movement and in theater," says Max Palevsky, "and I wanted to stage Antigone, which is about moral decisions. I wanted to cover the pool for people to sit on and stage the play in the living room."

"I started out using Mexican furniture — Craig almost had a heart attack."

167

Arthur Elrod House, 1968

John Lautner, Architect

"After showing me the site, Elrod said, 'Give me what you think I should have on this lot.' As a very knowledgeable interior designer, Elrod was capable of designing something really good for himself, but he wanted the architecturally exceptional," the late architect recounted in *John Lautner, Architect*.

Construction on Arthur Elrod's house began in 1968 with the roof, a conical concrete dome that consists of two slabs separated by a layer of insulation. The house perches on a narrow, rocky ridge south of Palm Springs, looking west to Mount San Jacinto and north to the town, and Lautner devised a concrete structure that hugs the rocky spine of the ridge and then bursts outward in a massive circular living room sixty feet in diameter. Lautner controlled the light and views with blades of glass — clerestory segments in the roof that he described as "radiating from the center like a desert flower." The electronically controlled segments offer slices of snow-capped mountains and sky. A deep overhang protects the interiors from the sun. Concrete cylinders set in the overhang hold low-voltage uplights. At night, the black slate floor disappears and the city lights become the focus.

Elrod was born in Georgia, studied at Chouinard Art School in Los Angeles, then went to work in San Francisco at W & J Sloane, where he met Harold Broderick. In 1954 Elrod and Broderick relocated from Beverly Hills to Palm Springs and opened Arthur Elrod Associates on Palm Canyon Drive, a design studio and furniture and fabric showroom. Elrod became the design king of the desert. He did second houses, third houses, spec houses, experimental houses, and hotels. Elrod was charming, handsome, and worked tirelessly for his A-list clientele. He hired talented associates — William Raiser and Steve Chase — and nurtured local artists and artisans.

For fifteen years Elrod had bought, renovated, and sold houses in the Las Palmas area, but he tired of that and finally decided to create something of his own. His design practice was flourishing — with the advent of jet travel he could expand his client base beyond the Palm Springs–Beverly Hills–Malibu axis to encompass Minneapolis, Houston, and Oklahoma. Now he was working on primary residences as well as the vacation houses. He had been named as one of America's top ten designers by *Time*. His projects were published extensively in shelter magazines. "Arthur was very correct and always called his clients Mr. and Mrs., at least until they paid him," says Paige Rense, editor-in-chief of *Architectural Digest*, where several of Elrod's projects were published in the 1960s and early 1970s, including his own house. "He was the one who persuaded them to look at their second or third house on a par with their primary residence. He made clients want to spend money on their weekend houses."

The curve of John Lautner's poured concrete roof looms out of a granite ledge on a ridge in the south edge of Palm Springs. "The more monolithic the better," Lautner said of the design.

Pages 170–171: Nine massive concrete beams radiate out from the living room's thirty-foot-high dome ceiling. Interior designer Steven Heisler, who is in the process of renovating the house for its current owner, re-created the round Edward Fields carpet as well as the Martin Brattrud arced sofa and curved bench.

172

Above: A screen of bamboo was planted to shield the sunken master bath from neighbors.
Upper left: A smaller concrete canopy covers the steel kitchen.
Far left: The original owner, designer Arthur Elrod, requested that Lautner incorporate the ridge's boulders in the interiors. "It was natural for the main living room to look over the desert and the bedroom wing should be back toward the street," said Lautner. Bottom left: Rock and tile form the guest bathroom.

"Arthur wanted a party house, and he got one."

"Arthur was very friendly with the Indians," says Broderick. "We bought the lot below, which was Indian land, and they allowed him to landscape it." The dynamic between designer and architect was also one of mutual respect. "Lautner called it the best furnished of his houses," says Broderick, who continued the design practice after Elrod's death.

"Arthur had tremendous enthusiasm but at the same time he could concentrate on the business at hand and get things done," said Lautner in a 1974 interview in the *Los Angeles Times*. "This was great for everyone on a project. But there was more than that. My relationship with him was exceptional. He was everything a client should be. He had an understanding of architecture and he was always open to new ideas. He never wanted to do the safe thing. He accepted my design and my recommendations entirely, and there was no interference. I think he was still maturing and developing when he died."

Lautner's resulting structure — he would refer to it later as "a million dollar sculpture" — resembles a concrete-and-glass mushroom that hovers overhead like a spaceship. Beyond hangar-like semicircular glass windows, the desert spreads itself out in a 220-degree view. The furniture was a mix of modernist pieces by Knoll, Harry Bertoia, Warren Platner, Marcel Breuer, and custom designs. A circular Edward Fields carpet of concentric circles woven in shades of green grounded the living room. A twenty-eight-foot arced sofa and facing curved bench by Martin Brattrud were covered in a Jack Lenor Larsen fabric stretched taut so that no seams showed. In the dining area the walls and buffet were of teak. Eight black leather and chrome chairs surrounded the dining table, which was six feet long with two sheets of three-quarter-inch black glass with hammered and polished edges on a glass-and-chrome base. "We had belly dancers performing on the table at one party," says Broderick.

A mitered glass wall that wrapped inside, around the living room's terrace, blew inward in a freak windstorm shortly before the house was to be used for the 1971 James Bond movie *Diamonds Are Forever*. "Doors flew off and the television set ended up in the middle of the Paul Jenkins artwork that had been specially stretched for the living room's arced wall," says Broderick. "We were supposed to be having a party for a hundred just two weeks after the storm. We ended up edging the floor with potted plants so that people didn't step off the rocks and into the pool." Lautner replaced the interior glass wall with massive electronic sliding glass doors suspended from the perimeter of the roof. The parties continued, and in fact became legendary. Bill Blass held a fashion show. *Playboy* did a feature. Elrod was photographed in his sunken bathtub afroth with bubbles. Neighbors included Steve McQueen and William Holden. "Arthur wanted a party house, and he got one," says Broderick.

Clerestory segments open the roof to slices of sky and allow the light to be manipulated. "Most people can't visualize what a house can be, so there's a lot of talk and changes and you lose the spark of your idea," said Lautner. "Here we talked maybe half an hour and I went ahead with it."

Above: Steps behind the living room lead past a Gene Flores water sculpture down to the guest wing, which was a later addition.

Right: From the master bedroom, stairs lead down to the pool. An original glass wall that wrapped inside blew out in a freak wind storm and was replaced by motorized glass windows suspended from the roof's perimeter.

Early one morning in February 1974 Elrod and his design associate Bill Raiser were driving to the office when their Fiat convertible was hit by a drunk driver. Both men were killed instantly. One of the projects they were working on at the time was a new house for Bob and Dolores Hope that Lautner had designed right above Elrod's. "The Hopes liked Arthur's house so much they built a larger version," says Broderick. "They would come to tea every Thursday for meetings. But the first house burned down and they had to start again."

Two years after Elrod died, Broderick, who still runs Arthur Elrod Associates, put the house on the market. It went through various owners and alterations until a recent restoration by Steven Heisler of Beckson Associates in Los Angeles returned much of its original spirit. •

Above: The sequence of circles starts at the circular motor court wall.
The roof is covered with plants; underneath are service areas.
Right: The sixty-foot living room floats above the desert, with a 220-degree view of the valley and the snow-capped San Jacinto Mountains.

Ambassador and Mrs. Walter H. Annenberg House, 1963

A. Quincy Jones and Frederick E. Emmons, Architects

Interior design: William Haines and Ted Graber

"By sketching on a trip I enhance my ability to see and feel spaces," wrote A. Quincy Jones in 1968 in the AIA *Journal*. His exquisitely rendered pen-and-ink drawings from his global travels always featured a strong vertical element, whether a conical hat worn by a vendor in Hong Kong, a kiln near Delhi, a grain elevator in Bangkok, or the religious spires of St. Petersburg, Manzanillo, and Kyoto. Jones, who taught architecture at the University of Southern California and in 1975 became its dean of architecture and fine arts, was always sensitive to the intense symbiosis between a structure and its site.

The vertical element in his ink-on-paper elevation, dated 11 August 1963, for the Rancho Mirage estate of Ambassador and Mrs. Walter H. Annenberg is a "monitor," a raised cupola of open fretwork that rises out of a Mayan-Japanese pyramid roof and gently illuminates the square atrium in the living room. "He liked a serious roof," wrote architecture critic Esther McCoy in her 1979 catalogue *A. Quincy Jones: A Tribute*.

Sunnylands, named after the Philadelphia estate of the ambassador's father, Moses Annenberg, sits on about 250 acres in Rancho Mirage near the intersection of Bob Hope and Frank Sinatra drives, protected by another two hundred acres of raw desert. "We bought the land in 1961, started planning in 1963, and moved in in 1966," says Lee Annenberg. "When we bought, Tamarisk Country Club was the only thing out here. A date ranch across the street became the Desert Island Golf Resort."

Oleander and eucalyptus were planted immediately around the perimeter to protect the vast tract that was going to be transformed from a "mountain of sand," in Lee Annenberg's words, into a green oasis that has rendered the desert moot. "There is no desert," she says. "The view looks like Switzerland — all green and mountains." The house radiates a soft pink from its roof, white from the loggia that wraps around it, and green from the surrounding rolling grassy terrain. Its color was dictated in part by the mountains to the east. "On summer evenings, those mountains are all pink; that's why we have a pink roof," she says.

Jones's first concept was to introduce water. "Quincy frequently drew buildings at the edge of a body of water. Structured form and its reflection were a preoccupation that may have begun in his years on the water in Seattle," wrote Ruth Weisberg, USC professor of fine arts, in the Japanese architecture magazine *Process*. A system of twelve lakes that provides watering holes for egrets and ducks winds through Sunnylands. "Walter, like Quincy, was very concerned with ecology and the environment and what civilizing this part of the desert would do to the water table," recalls the architect's widow and archivist, Elaine K. S. Jones. "He hired an expert on agronomy to make sure that they weren't hurting the water table and he bought a water tower nearby."

In front of the guest wing, an undulating sculpture by Yacov Agam and tilting umbrella shades highlight the pool at the Annenberg estate, Sunnylands.

At the same time that Dick Wilson, the best-known golf course architect of his time, was sculpting a nine-green, eighteen-tee, six-thousand-yard private golf course, architects A. Quincy Jones and partner Frederick E. Emmons and interior designers William Haines and Ted Graber were collaborating on the house. It had to have heft — it would be used constantly during the "season," from December to April, for entertaining royalty (Queen Elizabeth, Prince Philip, and Prince Charles), heads of state, and presidents (most frequently, Ronald Reagan) — and it had to provide a strong structural presence for outstanding collections of impressionist and postimpressionist art, oriental antiques, and Steuben glass without overwhelming them.

Quincy Jones and Billy Haines had worked together before, most notably between 1950 and 1952 on the modernist Holmby Hills house of Frances Brody, daughter of philanthropist Albert D. Lasker, and they respected each other's work. "You can't minimize the impact of an architect working with a decorator," Elaine Jones says. "Haines was crucial. And he didn't deny the building — he worked with it and never made any architectural recommendations."

"When Walter first took us out into that almost 250 acres of bare desert and tried to explain to Bill and me what he wanted, we both said, 'It sounds as if what you really want is an oasis,'" Ted Graber told *Town and Country* in February 1978. "Walter said, 'That's exactly what I want, and I don't want to see one grain of sand except in the golf traps.' Los Angeles architect Quincy Jones planned the house, which took more than two years to build. When we were almost finished Lee told us that she wanted the roof to be pink on the outside. Pink! That floored us. We were seeing the house from a masculine view, and she was thinking from a woman's standpoint. And she was right, because she has such a fantastic eye. You know how she wears that angelskin coral with an emerald-green dress? That's the effect."

Bottom left: The driveway leads into the motor court, which is surrounded by tightly trimmed ficus trees. Water splashes down the sides of the Maya column. A vertical "monitor," a raised cupola of open fretwork, rises out of Quincy Jones's Maya/Japanese-influenced roof.
Top left: From the front door, the coffered ceiling and inlaid marble floor define the 6,400-square-foot atrium that rises to 26 feet. At its tentlike center, the monitor casts soft light on an original cast of Rodin's Eve.
Above: The corner projection of the egg crate–ceilinged porte cochere faces the black bronze column, a copy of one at Mexico City's Museum of Anthropology, that sits on black riverbed pebbles.

Blending Mayan and Japanese influences, Jones drafted a 32,000-square-foot horizontal house topped by a sloping roof painted pink; the roofline and color repeat where the outdoor terrace slopes down into the pool. "Quincy Jones set a pink wall on the lake, like the prow of a ship," says Lee Annenberg, who had met the architect through her friend Frances Brody. "It's my favorite thing."

The drive up to the house passes by rolling hills and lakes into a courtyard, where tightly trimmed ficus planted in lava rock containers surround a black polished bronze Mayan column. Water splashes down the column onto black riverbed stones. A corner porte cochere with a coffered egg-crate ceiling leads into the coffered-ceiling atrium; at the center of the 26-foot-high room, which resembles a luxuriously appointed tent, sits the "monitor," filtering soft light over one of the original casts of Rodin's *Eve*. "The monitor is very deep, so it takes a long time for the light to travel down," notes Elaine Jones. Two walls of the 6,400-square-foot atrium are of square blocks of reddish-brown Mexican lava rock. The pink marble floor and walls painted in celadon allow the art to dominate. With the exception of a couple of antique cloisonne tables, Haines created the furniture for the entire house. He divided the atrium into various seating areas furnished with long chinoiserie-style cocktail

Above: Interior designers Billy Haines and Ted Graber divided the atrium into various sitting areas and custom-made all the furniture for the house—horizontal Chinese-style consoles, coffee tables, and Haines's signature hostess chair.

Left: A later wall addition of Mexican lava rock runs one length of the atrium and supports part of the Annenbergs' incredible collection of impressionist and postimpressionist paintings, among them works by Gauguin, Renoir, Picasso, and Van Gogh.

tables and chairs and his signature low-lying hostess chair. Card tables are of pale celadon leather with embossed-gold leather trim. A hallway to the right of the atrium leads down to the dining room, projection room, pool cabanas, and the guest suites. To the left lie the master wing and offices.

Every element of the structure, including the billowing tentlike ceiling, has a firm but silent aspect, animated by the presence of its inhabitants. "When you are designing a very fine house you must plan for the way people live in a fine home. The basics have to be planned very carefully. There are millions of details," Billy Haines told *Architectural Digest* in 1973, shortly before his death. "A house is a shell. The people who live in that house make it come alive, and no designer in the world can do that for them. They have to make it their home. They must possess the house. It should not possess them." •

"I don't want to see one grain of sand except in the golf traps."

Above: The pink roof is echoed where the loggia slips into the water outside the living room. "Quincy Jones set a pink wall on the lake, like the prow of a ship," says Lee Annenberg. "It's my favorite thing."

Left: A pink Chinese pagoda provides a resting spot for lunch on the Annenbergs' private nine-green, eighteen-tee golf course.

Right: The Annenbergs completely obliterated all traces of the sand dunes that had been there and replaced them with rolling hills, trees, and a connecting lake system more reminiscent of Europe than the California desert.

Overleaf: Egrets, both statues and the real thing, find shelter by one of seven lakes dug on the two-hundred-acre property. Ficus trees poke through the loggia, which wraps from the master wing around the living areas.

Bibliography

Note: *Palm Springs Villager* and *Palm Springs Life* magazines, the *Desert Sun* newspaper, and the Palm Springs Public Library provided extensive archival research material.

Ainsworth, Katherine. *The McCallum Saga*. Palm Springs: Palm Springs Desert Museum, 1973.

Bogert, Frank M. *Palm Springs: First Hundred Years*. Palm Springs: Palm Springs Heritage Associates, 1987.

Burke, Anthony. *Palm Springs, Why I Love You*. Palm Springs: Palmesa, 1978.

Chase, J. Smeaton. *Palm Springs, Our Araby: Palm Springs and the Garden of the Sun*. 1920. Reprint, Palm Springs: Palm Springs Library Board of Trustees, 1987.

Colacello, Bob. "Ronnie and Nancy." *Vanity Fair* (July 1998).

"Designer William Haines's Outspoken Comments." *Architectural Digest* (September/October 1973).

Escher, Frank, ed. *John Lautner, Architect*. London: Artemis, 1994.

Freiman, Ziva. "Back to Neutra." *Progressive Architecture* (November 1995).

Gardner, Ava. *Ava: My Story*. New York: Bantam, 1990.

Hines, Thomas S. *Richard Neutra and the Search for Modern Architecture*. New York: Oxford University Press, 1982.

Holmes, Nancy. "Barony in the Desert." *Town and Country* (February 1978).

"House of Steel." *Los Angeles Times Home Magazine* (13 May 1962).

Loewy, Raymond. *Industrial Design*. New York: Overlook Press, 1979.

—————. *Never Leave Well Enough Alone*. New York: Simon & Schuster, 1950.

MacMasters, Dan. "A Desert Home that Fits Its Environment." *Los Angeles Times Home Magazine* (1 December 1962).

—————. "Canopy of Concrete for Spectacular Desert House." *Los Angeles Times Home Magazine* (3 November 1968).

"La Maison realisée par Richard Neutra pour un collectioneur acquis aux arts actuels." *Connaissance des Arts* (March 1966).

McCoy, Esther. *Craig Ellwood: Architecture*. 1968. Reprint, Santa Monica, Ca.: Hennessy & Ingalls, 1997.

McKeller, Frank M. "New All-Steel Home System." *Home Builders Journal* (August 1962).

Miller, Dick. "Golfing's Golden Oasis." *Town and Country* (February 1981).

"Modern Palace in the Desert." *Architectural Digest* (Spring 1970).

Ouroussoff, Nicolai. "Retrieving the Future under a Desert Sky." *New York Times* (28 December 1995).

"Record Houses." *Architectural Record* (September 1963).

Richards, Elizabeth. *A Look into Palm Springs's Past.* Palm Springs: Santa Fe Federal Savings and Loan Association, 1961.

Rippingale, Sally Presley. *History of the Racquet Club of Palm Springs.* Palm Springs: U.S. Business Specialty, 1985.

Rosa, Joseph. *Albert Frey, Architect.* New York: Rizzoli International Publications, 1990.

Sewell, Elaine K., Ken Tanaka, and Katherine W. Rinne. "A. Quincy Jones: The Oneness of Architecture." *Process: Architecture* (October 1983).

Taylor, J. M. F. "William F. Cody: A Comment on Architecture." *Palm Springs Life* (August 1964).

Cocktails on the terrace of the Jorgensen House at Thunderbird
Country Club in Rancho Mirage. (see page 112)